THE BRIDE MAKES HERSELF READY

Aligned to the Plumb Line

TEACHER'S MANUAL

FAITH MARIE BACZKO

Faith Marie Baczko © Copyright 2020

Headstone Publishing
103-125 Forsythe St. Oakville Ontario L6K 3K1

All rights reserved.
This book is protected by the copyright laws of Canada.

This book may not be copied or reprinted for commercial gain or profit.

This book or portions thereof may not be reproduced stored in a retrieval system or transmitted in any form without prior written permission of the publisher.

All scripture quotations, unless otherwise indicated, are taken from the New King James Version®. Copyright © 1982 by Thomas Nelson, Inc. Used by permission. All rights reserved.

Scripture quotations marked (AMP) are taken from the Amplified Bible, Copyright © 1954, 1958, 1962, 1964, 1965, 1987 by The Lockman Foundation. Used by permission.

Scripture quotations marked (NIV) are taken from the Holy Bible, New International Version®, NIV®. Copyright © 1973, 1978, 1984 by Biblica, Inc.™ Used by permission of Zondervan. All rights reserved worldwide.
www.zondervan.com

All Hebrew and Greek translations are taken from the Strong's Exhaustive Concordance. Author: James Strong

ISBN - 9798546208264

Email: contact@headstoneministries.com
Website: www.headstoneministries.com

Cover and Interior design by Faith Marie Baczko
publishing@headstoneministries.com

Table of Contents

FAITH MARIE BACZKO	4
HEADSTONE INTERNATIONAL MINISTRIES	5
HEADSTONE ACADEMY	6
COURSE SPECIFICS	8
MODULE I: SPIRITUAL REALITIES	
INTRODUCTION	11
SESSION I: The Formation of Belief Systems	15
SESSION II: The Journey of Cleansing	32
SESSION III: He Has Nothing in Me	47
MODULE II: DELIVERANCE & RESET	
SESSION I: Forces Hindering Release	63
SESSION II: Cleansing the Bloodline I	77
SESSION III: Cleansing the Bloodline II	91
SESSION IV: Reprogramming the Brain	101
APPENDIX: Cleansing Prayers	109

FAITH MARIE BACZKO

PRESIDENT & FOUNDER OF HEADSTONE INTERNATIONAL MINISTRIES

In 1993 Faith Marie Baczko had a life-transforming encounter with the Lord at her apartment in downtown Toronto. In obedience to the Lord, she walked away from her career as a fashion designer, and the store she had recently opened in the heart of Toronto. When she asked the Lord what she would do, He said, "Write." Though having no experience in writing, and no natural ability, something was awakened in Faith, she believed God and chose to follow Him.

With her twelve-year-old son Jesse, Faith followed the Lord to a small village outside of Toronto. There the Lord began her training and the cleansing of her soul in His refining fire; there also He began to teach her about His House, and the completing work on His House— the Headstone or Capstone. After losing her son in a tragic car accident in 2006, Faith married her husband Frank and launched Headstone International Ministries.

Faith Marie Baczko is presently the President of *HIM* and *Headstone Academy*; Ministries that are rich and robust in the purposes and plans of God. She has an entrepreneurial, pioneering spirit that moves her to continually break new ground. Faith is a prophetic teacher, bringing significant revelation to mobilize, equip and strengthen the Body of Christ for this momentous hour of history. Faith is a member of *Catch the Fire Leaders Alliance* and is a member of BAMN – *Breakthrough Apostolic Ministries Network*, under the leadership of Apostle Barbara Yoder.

Faith carries key insights into the profound significance of Israel's place in the purposes of God, and in the summing up of all things in Christ. She is an author and regular contributor to the Elijah List prophetic ministry; she is also an international speaker and has held many Conferences and Schools in South America developing enduring relationships with pastors and leaders. Faith has a deep desire for the Army of God to Arise with passion and power and models a life that inspires others to live rigorously devoted to passionately pursuing Christ. Her books are now all available in Spanish.

Faith is available to speak at churches, and to hold Schools & Seminars focused on:

- Discovering the dynamics of our God-given identity in Christ for 'Such a time.'
- The significance of Israel in God's purposes & plans
- The significance of God's plan for women in the last days
- Becoming a Bride ready for the Master

HEADSTONE INTERNATIONAL MINISTRIES © FAITH MARIE BACZKO

HEADSTONE INTERNATIONAL MINISTRIES

Headstone International Ministries has been created and established to offer to the Christian Church of any denomination, courses reflecting important facets of *the Headstone*. The foundation for all our books, courses and, resources is the revelation the Lord gave on the Headstone—*His completing work in His people and His House*. Participation in our resources, therefore, requires a certain level of understanding of the dynamics of the Headstone.

The Headstone is the final stone that completes the House of God. It brilliantly showcases facets of the ultimate and priceless Gemstone that is our God—facets He will have restored and presented in its fullness and reflected in the House prepared for Jesus' return.

The Headstone or Capstone of the temple of God represents the perfecting work of God in His people to bring them into the fullness of the Glory and majesty of Christ. The Headstone corresponds to the Holy of Holies—the Sanctuary the Holy Spirit is preparing for the Lord's return, to host the Ark of His Presence. It embodies a generation called forth for such a time, to carry the weight of His Glory and to prepare His way for His return. For a more in-depth analysis on this subject, our course—*The Headstone*, delivers a comprehensive study on this subject.

The mandate of this Ministry is to equip and prepare the saints for the specific period in history referred to in the Bible as, *the times of the summing up of all things in Christ*—a period we are presently entering. This is a time that will ultimately culminate in the Return of our Lord Jesus Christ.

Marked by wars and rumors of wars, with great shaking occurring in the earth in every sphere of life, this epoch will be turbulent and volatile. The tumult of this hour in history will demand that a high caliber of authentic apostolic and prophetic leadership begin to arise, along with a radical passionate apostolic army of lovers of God, (2 Pet. 3:11). For the true and authentic Church of God, this time will be its greatest hour, a season marked by God's Glory, Love, and Power!

The Headstone Army of God—that are the sons of God, will be brought forth in travail to serve the purposes of the King, to complete His last Day campaign for the restoration of all things to His original intention!

"He shall bring forth the Headstone with shoutings, crying, Grace, Grace to it!"

HEADSTONE ACADEMY

Thank you for your decision to participate in a Headstone Academy Course. We are a ministry providing cutting-edge courses prepared for and tailored to this hour of history and we believe you will be blessed by our resources.

We are presently living in very unusual times in the history of the Church and of the world, times fraught with awe and wonder. Times where we have seen God move in fresh and unique ways and on scales not previously seen. The last two decades were characterized by powerful moves of God in many nations of the Earth as momentum builds. The Bible teaches there are seasons appointed to every purpose of God, each designed to continually move us forward and closer to the day of His coming and the Kingdom age.

The Scriptures use the term *the fullness of time* to describe the period surrounding the closing of one season and the transition into another. There are numerous signs unique to the last 100 years in the history of the Church that help us to discern the times we are living in. These signs, when viewed together as a whole indicate that we have arrived at a milestone and a volatile period of history propelling us intentionally toward the birth of a new era.

I believe that God has timed to the hour the moment when seasons change, and we are transported into new and appointed times. Our Schools are intentionally focused on this season God calls the *fullness of time*. This period is related to:

- The completion of God's work in man
- The completion of God's House begun in Israel, that will be completed in Israel
- This *kairos* appointed *season of completion* before the rapture takes place

The Headstone is a prepared **Sanctuary** consistent with the nature of Christ, representing the **fullness of Christ** in the **fullness of time**. We are moving toward something wondrous!

> **Ephesians 4:13** *"..until we all reach unity in the faith and in the knowledge of the Son of God and become mature, **attaining to the whole measure of the fullness of Christ.***

> **Ephesians 1:10** *"...that in the **dispensation of the fullness of times** He might gather in one all things in Christ both which are in heaven and which are on earth—in Him."*

OUR COURSES

Our courses are a collective body of teaching embedded with significant revelation for this present crucial hour of history. All courses were prepared, written, and produced by Faith Marie Baczko and were received by revelation. These are teachings vital to our service to the Lord *in preparation for the Day that He returns!* Our Courses are in-depth studies on facets of the

Sanctuary God is now preparing, referred to as the Headstone of the House of God according to Zechariah 4:7. We believe this is the Sanctuary now being prepared to host Jesus in His fullness.

This sanctuary is comprised of seven facets—of course, there are numerous features to the House of God not covered in these courses, taught by many anointed teachers who specialize in those areas; however, they will fall within the umbrella of these seven facets:

- An Apostolic people clothed in power
- Women created in His image
- An Army prepared for service,
- The Bride prepared in purity and holiness.
- The Headstone—completion of the House of God and an army prepared for fullness
- The Healing River providing cleansing and Deliverance for God's people
- God's transcendent plan in and through Israel

These are all key features; however, we do feel that the most important body of teaching we are called to take to the nations, is regarding Israel. Our course, *For the Cause of Zion*, contains truths that are vital to the Body of Christ and the health and welfare of all nations.

As these resources pertain to the closing chapter of this age, some may be interested in our thoughts on where we stand regarding the rapture. Our position is this: there are many points of view on the timing of the rapture that has taken on an obsessive dynamic, sourced in a religious spirit that seeks to divide and has caused much offense in the family of God. The only Scripture that mentions this phenomenon, tells us that it takes place at the sound of the last trumpet ...*whenever that may be* (1 Cor. 15:22). Our courses are all intentionally focused on the dispensation of the fullness of times—the season *preceding the rapture*. So hopefully all can find common ground to agree as we focus on the work to be presently done.

We do not know how much time God has given to prepare the way for the coming of the Bridegroom King, but *whatever* time He has given us is to be used wisely, and the time to begin is *now! The Kingdom of Heaven is at hand*, which is to say it is *fast approaching*! Please enjoy the course.

Yours in Christ.

Faith Marie Baczko

President & Founder – Headstone International Ministries

COURSE SPECIFICS

The Bride Makes Herself Ready course is comprised of six Sessions. Each Session should take approximately 45-60 minutes. We suggest that you leave time to allow for discussion and questions at the end, and for prayer and ministry time.

Course Materials Available for purchase:

1. PowerPoints Video Presentation for those teaching the material
2. Teachers Manual
3. Student Manual (also included with online Course)
4. Some Courses and certain Sessions may come with PDF documents to download. If so, these PDF Notes will be made available in the Appendices of the Manuals

Please Note: We strongly encourage you to complete this Course before taking any other Courses as it will take you through a process of heart cleansing that will give you greater ability to hear the Holy Spirit and process revelation. It will change your life!

All Materials are available for purchase as a download on our Store at:

store.headstoneministries.com

Manuals are also available for purchase on Amazon.com

(If purchased on Amazon we suggest having the binding changed to a spiral binding for easier management of manual)

MODULE I:
SPIRITUAL REALITIES

Introduction

Faith Marie Baczko

Many years ago, as I was praying in preparation to teach a Bible study, the Lord showed me a picture. I saw a large and high tower stretching into the sky. Covering the tower were numerous doors and windows of all shapes and sizes—they were all open. As I stared at the tower, each one began to slam shut. At the same time, I heard the distant sound of marching from an approaching army, and I received the understanding that this study was to be concerned with the preparation and transformation of willing servants into towers of refuge for the battles ahead. The Lord highlighted the importance of closing gates to the enemy as an important part of training and preparation for the battles to prepare the way for the Return of the King. Isaiah 32:1-2 provides an astonishing view of God's ultimate intention to fashion a man in the image of Himself:

> **"Behold, a king will reign in righteousness, and princes will rule with justice. A man will be as a hiding place from the wind, and a cover from the tempest, as rivers of water in a dry place, as the shadow of a great rock in a weary land."**

At the time of our salvation and entrance into the kingdom of God, we are launched with the Holy Spirit on the journey of a lifetime, a journey of transformation into Christlikeness and conformity to His image. This is a process the Bible refers to as Sanctification. All children of God are on this journey, at different stages of the process. Falling in love with Jesus and spending intimate time in His Presence greatly speeds up the process of conformation, as we are *'changed in His Presence.'* The Father's determination is that our minds be transformed and renewed to become like His Son's—that we would live a Christ-centered life, positioned in His will where we are kept safe and protected. It is therefore of utmost importance to walk closely with the Holy Spirit, allow Him to teach us the ways and principles of God, and direct our paths.

Jesus is the Plumb Line the Father uses to test all measures and standards pertaining to His House. Jesus' Life force is the gravitational pull that forever works to draw all things into alignment and conformity to God! God uses the Plumb Line of Jesus—the *Word of God incarnate*, as the foundation of His temple and as the measure of its growth as it is built upward rising in Glory to the Stature of Christ (Eph. 4:13).

In the process of being conformed to Christ's image, all children of God will embark on the journey toward Christlikeness and the Glory of God, in their growth toward spiritual maturity. I pray that this Course will be beneficial to you on this journey to becoming a mature son or daughter of God.

It grieves the Father when we choose to entertain sin in His House consciously or unconsciously as sin leads to defeat, and *it especially grieves Him to see His enemies having victory over His children!*

This Course seeks to bring revelation of tactics the enemy has so far used very successfully to defile the House of God and defeat the saints of God. The intended aim is to bring the revelation needed for saints to become safe vessels in the Lord's army. We must aspire to become *vessels of gold safe or fit for the Master to use; to be* safe within ourselves, safe to others in our church and safe to those on our team (2 Tim. 2:20).

Being cleansed of the ways of the world we have come out of, and the attitudes and mindsets we had acquired over a lifetime, is a vital process to our wellbeing. This will be especially important during the turmoil and shakings the earth is and will continue to experience. These un-Christlike ways and min prevent us from appropriating truth, and from receiving clear direction from the Lord. This Course intends to be an aid in the development of the Bride's growth as we mature and grow up to the measure of the fullness of Christ!

This Course provides valuable understanding and revelation to the saints of God—vital information that may not have been previously known or presented in such a way as to bring enlightenment. It opens to us choices that will transform our spiritual life and daily walk with God. *It* calls attention to gates the enemy uses to harass, oppress, and hinder the saints of God to ultimately steal their destinies in Christ.

There is no condemnation for those who are in Christ; His love for us is unconditional and His desire is for us to live the abundant life He died to give us! It is important to note that in the process of sanctification and our walk with the Lord, He will never overwhelm us with the issues of our heart; He will deal with each issue in His loving way and in His perfect time.

The following are some important points to take note of and keep in mind as you walk through the pages of this book, as the enemy of your soul likes to take the good things God wants to do in and through us to get us off-balanced. The teachings of this book are not:

- A means of perfecting the soul in a quest to *attain salvation.*
- Advocating perfecting the soul through *works* apart from the finished work of Christ accomplished at the Cross.
- This teaching does not adhere to any means of deliverance other than by repentance through the Blood of Jesus Christ.
- Our intention is not to promote spiritual superiority, to raise anyone above others in a prideful way. *True growth and maturity will always take you to the lowest place in brokenness before God!*

- The intention is not to advocate excessive self-examination. The leading of the Holy Spirit—His timing and His direction in the process of sanctification—*is emphasized.*

These are all traps the enemy will set on the path of those who would go on with the Lord to serve Him. This Course should not be approached in the religious spirit characterized by the law—*striving to keep rules and regulations!* Each chapter should be approached as *an invitation to surrender* and give Christ His place to become all, in and through you!

Jesus Christ is *the Plumb Line* of the Temple of God; He is *the Blueprint* of the House of God we will therefore follow in this study. Jesus is the vision we will keep in view as we look at the gates into our souls and the Temple that is the Body of Christ. Our focus on Christ will help us to:

- Magnify the Lord in our understanding that He is Lord and Savior.
- Begin to understand ourselves, and the roots of habitual sin.
- Identify the gates giving the enemy access to our lives.
- CLOSE THESE GATES.
- Become united with Christ in heart and mind as we exchange our 'stuff' for His 'Life' and allow His life to increase within us.

"Do you not know that you are the temple of God and that the Spirit of God dwells in you." 1 Corinthians 3:16

This course will be beneficial to all saints, but it is especially important for the safety of those who are on the frontlines to have such teaching made available to them, as they become prime targets of the enemy.

This Course is an excellent tool an individual can use to take themselves through the process of cleansing and deliverance; when used as a group study there can be a greater impact, as there is the added power of agreement and confession.

God has supplied us with the tools to equip us for the battles we will surely encounter during the trials and testing of our faith to guarantee our arrival at the finish line as victorious saints.

"Let us purify ourselves from everything that contaminates body and spirit. Perfecting holiness out of reverence for God." 2 Corinthians 7:1 NIV

SESSION I:
THE FORMATION OF BELIEF SYSTEMS

Biblical Foundation

Slide 1: 2 Corinthians 4:18 "...while we do not look at the things which are seen, <u>but at the things which are not seen.</u> For the things which are seen are temporary, but the things which are not seen are eternal."

Slide 2:

WHAT IS TRUTH?

1. The answer to this question reveals the condition of our foundation and will determine the course of one's life! This question must therefore be settled at the beginning of our Journey with the Lord.

2. The world's present view: *"Tolerance and commonality of spiritual consciousness is the order of the day. No one has a monopoly on truth. You must find <u>your own truth</u>..."*

3. This statement reflects the way the world presently thinks and has given birth to the concept of <u>political correctness, inclusiveness</u> and a wide range of beliefs that are now directing the course of societies around the world to its peril.

4. This statement is diametrically opposed to the Word of God, which embodies the reality that <u>the source of *truth* is not a human being</u>—this cannot be, as we are *the created*—not *the Creator*.

   Romans 1: 25 "They exchanged the truth of God for a lie and worshiped and <u>served created things rather than the Creator</u>—who is forever praised. Amen."

5. It is impossible for a created being to be the <u>source of anything</u> related to truth, reality, and life, as we are on the receiving end of truth and all revelation comes from above.

6. God, the Creator of *all things*, can be the only <u>source of truth</u>! He imparts absolute truth—we choose to receive it or not.

Slide 3:

THE POWER OF THE WORD OF GOD

1. The Word of God is truth. Truth can only be found within the <u>Author of Truth</u>—*the Word of God made flesh—Jesus Christ* (John 1).

2. God's Word is living and supernatural—the Holy Spirit inhabits God's Word, releasing the power for His Word to accomplish <u>whatever is desired</u>:

   Isaiah 55:11 "So shall My word be that goes forth from My mouth; it shall not return to Me void, but it shall <u>accomplish what I please,</u> and it shall prosper in the thing for which I sent it."

3. Nothing can withstand the determination of God! All obstacles in the path of God's Word, plan, purposes and will, must give way to <u>the power of His will</u>, *and fall before Him.*

   Jeremiah 23:29 "Is not My word like a fire?" says the LORD, "And like a hammer that breaks the rock in pieces?"

4. The Word of God is supernatural and powerful; by faith, God gives us the authority to declare His Word and call forth into our reality the things <u>that do not yet exist</u>, to transform our world!

___

Slide 4:

THE POWER OF THE WORD OF GOD

1. God's Word is also the <u>food and sustenance</u> of His people; it nourishes us and causes us to grow in wisdom, providing the strength to stand in any situation.

   Psalm 119:28 "My soul melts from heaviness; strengthen me <u>according to Your word</u>"

2. God uses His Word for direction to guide us in our call toward His intended destination. Our wonderful Father directs our steps by <u>illuminating the path</u> ahead of us with His Word.

   Psalm 119:105: "Your word is a lamp to my feet and a <u>light to my path</u>."
   Ps. 133: "Direct my steps <u>by Your word</u>, and let no iniquity have dominion over me"

3. Jesus came to preach *Good news—the truth* that would <u>set the captives free</u>. According to His Word, Jesus came to heal the brokenhearted, release those bound in prisons, console those who mourn, give them beauty for ashes, give sight to the blind and health to the sick (Isaiah 61).

Slide 5:

THE POWER OF THE WORD OF GOD

1. Jesus came as the Light of truth to expose the *lie,* and satan—*the father of lies,* and to destroy the <u>works of darkness</u>.

   John 8:44 "You are of *your* father the devil, and the desires of your father you want to do. He was a murderer from the beginning, and does not stand in the truth, because <u>there is no truth in him</u>. When he speaks a lie, he speaks from his own *resources,* for he is a liar and the father of it."

   1 John 3:8: "For this purpose the Son of God was manifested, that He might <u>destroy the works of the devil.</u>"

Slide 6:

UNDERSTANDING THE SPIRITUAL DYNAMIC

1. The world's way of thinking is devoid in the understanding that there is a spiritual dynamic to life; one that includes realms with entities vying for power and dominion over the minds and thoughts of mankind.

   2 Corinthians 10:3-5: "For though we walk in the flesh, we do not war according to the flesh. For the weapons of our warfare are not carnal but mighty in God for <u>pulling down strongholds, casting down arguments and every high thing that exalts itself against the knowledge of God</u>, bringing every thought into captivity to the obedience of Christ..."

THE BRIDE MAKES HERSELF READY

2. Humanity occupies the natural world but has been given the capacity through our spirit to access the spiritual realms.

3. Just as significant, especially to the well-being of humanity, is the fact that our world is easily accessed by entities from other realms.

4. However, to true seekers of truth, God has provided in His Word, the knowledge and understanding of the government, character, and administrations of the spiritual realms and those who occupy them, and the ability to be victorious over their evil schemes.

Slide 7:

UNDERSTANDING THE SPIRITUAL DYNAMIC

1. Created human beings inhabit the natural realm, each possessing a physical body that will one day disintegrate, however, having a spirit and soul that is eternal.

   1 Thessalonians 5:23 "Now may the God of peace Himself sanctify you completely; and may your whole spirit, soul, and body be preserved blameless at the coming of our Lord Jesus Christ."

2. The natural realm will one day pass away, but the spiritual realm is eternal.

   1 Corinthians 15:3 "For this corruptible must put on incorruption, and this mortal must put on immortality"

Slide 8:

UNDERSTANDING THE SPIRITUAL DYNAMIC

1. Distinct entities having personality live in the spirit realms. The entities from the dominion of Light are angels, archangels, seraphim, and cherubim. These all bow in worship and in service to the Trinity of Father, Son, and Holy Spirit, and abide in the third heaven (2 Cor. 12:2).

Revelations 7:11: "<u>All the angels were standing around the throne</u> and around the elders and the four living creatures. They fell down on their faces before the throne and worshiped God…"

Slide 9:

UNDERSTANDING THE SPIRITUAL DYNAMIC

1. The dominion of darkness is occupied by an organized hierarchy of ruling principalities and powers influencing <u>cities, nations and peoples</u>—a demonic host having *evil intent*. They were thrown out of Heaven, function in the realms below the third heaven, and have authority in the sphere of sin.

   Ephesians: 6:12 "**For our struggle is not against flesh and blood, but against the rulers, against the authorities, against the powers of this dark world and against the <u>spiritual forces of evil in</u> the heavenly realms.**"

Slide 10:

UNDERSTANDING THE SPIRITUAL DYNAMIC

1. Satan, who is the *prince of the power of the air,* along with his demonic hosts works aggressively and relentlessly to distort all communication between the realms, <u>not protected by the Blood</u> of Jesus (Eph. 2:2).

2. In a future time, Satan will be thrown down to Earth from the second heaven; he will take possession of a governmental ruler and seize control of the world

   2 Thessalonians 2:10 "**The coming of the lawless one is according to the working of Satan, <u>with all power, signs, and lying wonders, and with all unrighteous deception</u> among those who perish, because they did not receive <u>the love of the truth</u>, that they might be saved.**" (see also Rev. 12).

3. An understanding of the spiritual realms, the ground rules of interaction between these realms and our world, and the determination of the rulers *of these realms,* is therefore a necessary factor in the process of making the right choices—*choices that can sometimes mean life or death.*

   Colossians 3:1-2 "If then you were raised with Christ, seek those things which are above, where Christ is, sitting at the right hand of God. Set your mind on things above, not on things on the earth."

Slide 11:

THE FORMATION OF BELIEF SYSTEMS

1. Humanity's understanding and knowledge of life c only from information *it has* received! Humanity's belief system is fashioned from the accumulation of information gathered through the senses.

2. This information is then shaped within individuals over a lifetime, from seven main sources:

   1. Our Experiences (both good and bad)

   2. Our Culture—the culture of the nation we were born into

   3. Our Community—where we live

   4. Incomplete, distorted, or manipulated data and information, that we are bombarded with daily.

   5. Malevolent spiritual entities intent on deception—continually feeding people with lies.

   6. Ungodly beliefs and misguided faith—these work together powerfully to produce a false reality:

      Hebrews 11:1 "Now faith is the substance of things hoped for, the evidence of things not seen"

   7. The Spirit of God, and the Word of God—for both Christians and the secular world

Slide 12:

THE FORMATION OF BELIEF SYSTEMS

1. Psychics, mediums, and people who have opened their soul to the spiritual realm do receive information and have communication with these realms, but the source is demonically inspired, <u>having evil intent</u>:

   John 10:10: "The thief does not come <u>except to steal, and to kill, and to destroy</u>. I have come that they may have life, and that they may have it more abundantly"

2. Without the intervention of God's mercy, released through the Grace of Jesus Christ, the world is caught in this <u>contrived trap of deception.</u>

   2 Thessalonians 2:10-12 ".... because they did not receive <u>the love of the truth</u>, that they might be saved. And for this reason, God will send them strong delusion, that they should believe the lie, that they all may be condemned who did not believe the truth but had pleasure in unrighteousness."

Slide 13:

THE BATTLE OVER WHO IS LORD?

1. Let us look at the <u>soul and the brain</u> in relation to the formation of belief systems:

   Romans 8:5-7: "For those who live according to the flesh, set their minds on the things of the flesh, but those who live according to the Spirit, the things of the Spirit. For to be carnally minded is death, but to be Spiritually minded is life and peace. <u>Because the carnal mind is enmity against God</u>, for it is not subject to the law of God, nor indeed can be."

2. God created the soul and the supercomputer we call the brain to be the *servant* of man's spirit—the spirit being the place of communion between God and man, and for the Christian, <u>the seat of His throne.</u>

Slide 14:

WHO IS LORD?

1. From the moment of birth, the brain is <u>continually receiving</u>, processing, and wrestling with the information it has received from three main sources:

    1) The senses—<u>sight, hearing, taste, touch, smell</u>

    2) The soul—*mind, will and emotions*

    3) Spiritual realm—<u>whether good or evil</u>

2. Based on the choice of what is believed, the brain will work to produce for the individual, <u>a worldview</u>.

    Romans 7:22-25 "For I delight in the law of God according to <u>the inward man</u>. But I see another law in my members, warring against the <u>law of my mind, and bringing me into captivity to the law of sin.</u>

___

Slide 15:

WHO IS LORD?

1. The personality is shaped by the soul—*the mind, will, and emotions,* from <u>the brain's perception</u> of the soul's beliefs, based on the information it has received through the senses over its lifetime.

2. For the world and for many Christians, <u>the soul through intellect has become</u> *master*.

    Proverbs 16:9: "A man's heart plans his way, but the Lord directs his steps"

3. Conclusions, *whether true or false* are recorded in the brain. Our will, our attitude, and our speech will reflect our core beliefs and conclusions formed and registered in the brain.

4. The brain *serves our beliefs* whether they are Godly and true, or ungodly and false!

5. An ungodly belief is any belief that is <u>not in agreement with the Word of God</u> or aligned to the principles of God—*a belief that exalts itself above the truth and knowledge of God (2 Cor. 10:5).*

THE FORMATION OF BELIEF SYSTEMS

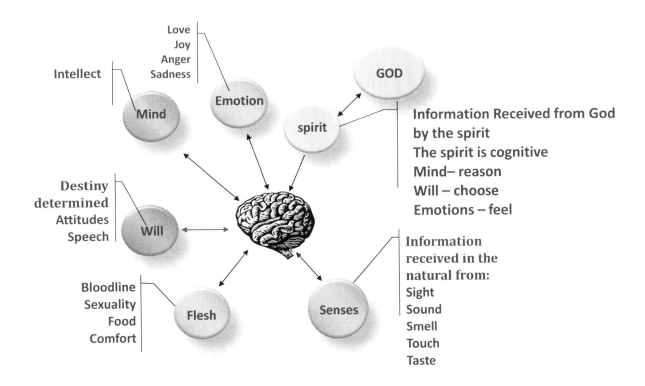

6. It is especially important to understand that the soul does not have the ability to discern spiritually, and therefore, does not have access to revelation necessary to make wise God-ordained choices based on truth!

7. The soul will draw conclusions and make choices <u>based on intellect,</u> carnal reasoning, or emotion—or on conscience if trained in an environment of right thinking.

___

Slide 16: WHO IS THE LORD OF YOUR LIFE

1. Who will you choose to be the Lord of your life? Will it be:

    ➢ **Jesus:** <u>through the Holy Spirit?</u>

    ➢ **Your Emotions:** <u>anger, sadness, offense unforgiveness, love</u>

    ➢ **Your Mind:** <u>Intellect</u>

    ➢ **Your Will:** <u>Independence, Attitudes, speech</u>

    ➢ **Your Senses:** <u>sight, sound, smell, touch, taste</u>

    ➢ **Your Flesh**: <u>Generational Bloodline & ways, Sexuality, food, Comfort</u>

2. Your decision is very important to the level of victory you will get from this course, as any gains made outside of Christ have no valid foundation and will be easily stolen—then you are back at square one or even worse.

3. Many people struggle with the same issues over a lifetime, never fully getting the victory. This is the product of cracks in the foundation, or gates that remain open to your soul.

Slide 17:

THE BELIEF EXPECTATION CYCLE

1. Because what we believe is so important, we need to understand how ungodly beliefs work against us. The economy of the spiritual realm is founded on faith. Faith gives you purchasing power.

   Hebrews 11:1 "Faith is the substance of things hoped for the evidence of things not seen."

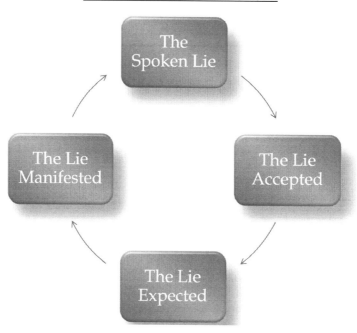

2. Through misguided faith, a person's beliefs become 'substance' and will become 'evidence' by the law of attraction, drawing circumstances and experiences to affirm his beliefs, and therefore shape his life and his destiny whether negatively or positively (Heb. 11:1). This is sometimes called the belief-expectation cycle.

3. If the Spoken lie becomes a lie that is accepted, it will in turn become a lie that is expected and will ultimately become a lie that is manifested.

4. For example, a child may possess a perfectly healthy brain, capable of incredible genius; nevertheless, if that child has been told repeatedly by an authority figure, such as a parent, a teacher or a pastor, that he will never amount to anything, should the child <u>receive these words as truth</u>, these declarations will form ungodly beliefs that work to cripple the child's future and destiny.

5. The un-Godly beliefs will become <u>his truth</u> even though the real truth is that God has fashioned the child with massive potential to achieve success and impossibilities.

6. <u>The spoken lie is given power</u> and ultimately becomes a curse that steals the child's potential, the wonderful possibilities of his life, and his true destiny in God.

7. The child's brain will accept his conclusions, and therefore, <u>*his expectations about himself*</u>, and like a good servant will work extremely hard, with the help of oppressive spiritual entities, to <u>produce the fruit of his false beliefs</u>.

8. Every action first begins with a thought; over time, if an action is repeated often, undergirded, and reinforced by ungodly beliefs, it will become a pattern with the potential to produce a stronghold in one's life

___

___

___

Slide 18:

THE BELIEF EXPECTATION CYCLE

1. Diabolical spiritual entities will then support the process, by continually working to plant thoughts that <u>reinforce these ungodly beliefs</u> over a person's lifetime, successfully keeping them bound in captivity to lies.

   Acts 26:18 "I am sending you to them to <u>open their eyes and turn them from darkness to light, and from the power of Satan to God</u>, so that they may receive forgiveness of sins and a place among those who are sanctified by faith in me."

2. Whenever the enemy gains access to our lives, he will seek to establish strongholds of stubbornness, arrogance, and deception where he is able to remain hidden from view behind the <u>armor of pride</u>—there he works to undermine the foundation of righteousness that God seeks to establish in our lives.

3. When we believe lies, we form a pact with the enemy. We give them a place in our souls to begin to <u>build a belief system</u>, where they can wage war against our souls and build strongholds that cause addictions to sexual sin, pornography, new age beliefs, financial iniquity, gluttony, argumentativeness, judgmental attitudes and many more.

___

___

___

Slide 19:

PROPAGANDA & LIES

1. God cautions us in His Word not to drink (intake) from broken cisterns, these are demonically inspired thoughts or words. We are to drink only from the LORD—*the Fountain of Life.*

   Jeremiah 2:13 "For My people have committed two evils: they have forsaken Me, <u>the fountain of living waters,</u> *and* hewn themselves cisterns—broken cisterns that can hold no water.

2. Propaganda works as a powerful tool, as it reinforces a lie *<u>through repetition.</u>* No one is exempt from falling into this trap, except for those who <u>walk closely with the Lord</u>, who are led by the Holy Spirit and hear His Voice.

   Propaganda: *the deliberate spreading of information and ideas propagated by an organization, government, or movement to establish their purposes for their benefit, or to bring harm.*

3. This explains the battle over fake news the world is now experiencing. People, or even whole societies, will accept a lie as the truth when it is told repeatedly over time. This has been proven through numerous instances over History.

4. For example, Hitler's demonic propaganda regarding the Jews, and the present attempt by certain nations to <u>re-write history</u> denying the Holocaust in their schoolbooks.

5. Germans were well-educated people, yet they chose to believe the lies and the propaganda and followed an insane leader on a disastrous path.

6. Man's beliefs apart from the Word and determination of God, <u>*are therefore not truth at all,*</u> but rather, simply a collection of thoughts, feelings, and ideas that have shaped his life and his thinking.

THE FORMATION OF BELIEF SYSTEMS

Slide 20:

THE SPIRIT MAN & TRUTH

1. Truth, revelation, and understanding come from God by His Spirit, through to our spirit man. Our natural intellect then processes the information to form <u>Godly conclusions founded on truth.</u>

    Proverbs 20:27 "<u>The spirit of a man is the lamp of the LORD</u>, searching all the inner depths of his heart."

2. The spirit given to man by God is cognitive at conception, possessing the ability to reason, choose and feel—having mind, will and emotions—<u>*apart from*</u> the natural body's mind, will and emotions:

    Jeremiah 1:5 "Before I formed you in the womb, <u>I knew you</u>..."

3. It has been proven that while in the womb, babies can hear and understand in ways <u>science states,</u> they are not able to.

    Job 32:7-8 "...Age should speak, and multitude of years should teach wisdom.' But <u>there is a spirit in man, and the breath of the Almighty gives him understanding.</u>"

4. God designed communion with Himself to be <u>through our spirit man</u>—*Spirit to spirit*—not Spirit to brain (as was shown in the diagram), '*deep calls unto deep*' (Ps. 42:7).

Slide 21:

A VEIL OF DECEPTION OVER THE WORLD

1. The veil of deception presently covering the mind of humanity, is removed *only* as the Life of Christ enters the spirit of man, and <u>*His Light of truth*</u> shines into the darkness of deception!

2. This veil of deception has worked to create <u>a prison that keeps humanity bound</u> in a world of lies and deception.

   2 Corinthians 3:14-16 "But their minds were blinded. For until this day the same veil remains un-lifted... <u>because the veil is taken away in Christ</u>... Nevertheless, when one turns to the Lord, the veil is taken away."

3. Apart from God, the other six sources of information received, (spoken of earlier) have all worked together to give birth to the many *so-called* 'truths,' religions, cults and philosophies espoused in the world throughout history.

4. Today, there is a smorgasbord of religions and philosophies offered from malevolent sources disguised with benevolence; any of which a man can choose to fit his worldview and to suit his personal lifestyle—the emphasis is <u>on *oneself*</u> rather than *on truth*!

Slide 22:

THE *WAY* THE *TRUTH* AND THE *LIFE*

1. *Jesus alone is the source of truth!* Because God in His wisdom was mindful that crooked thought patterns would develop in man's soul from demonic oppression, producing error and deception, He gave us His written Word, and He gave us Jesus as the Plumb Line and <u>the Standard by which we could measure</u> *truth*.

   Hebrews 1:1 "God, who at various times and in various ways spoke in time past to the fathers by the prophets, has in these last days spoken to us by His Son, whom He has appointed heir of all things, through whom also He made the worlds..."

2. God now communicates to His children by the Holy Spirit through the Life of His Son. Our thoughts must be <u>purified by the Cross</u> to reflect the standard of the Plumb line of Jesus Christ and to have the ability to hear and understand a clear word of truth from heaven.

3. Jesus, in whom truth finds its existence, can be the *only* source in the search for truth, the *only* standard by which we can measure right and wrong, and the *only* Light in determining <u>a course of action</u>:

   John 14:6 "I am the way, the truth, and the life. <u>No one comes to the Father except through Me."</u>

4. Jesus, as the *One who paid the full penalty for the sin of humanity*, re-opened the door of communication with God the Father (Heb. 1:2).

5. The demonic realm can manipulate and distort truth and spread its lies through those who seek information <u>outside of God</u>.

6. Mediums, psychics, and philosophers may appear <u>as angels of light</u> bringing comfort and hope to seekers, but their words are empty, used simply to pull the ignorant into their deadly trap.

Slide 23:

THE *WAY* THE *TRUTH* AND THE *LIFE*

1. Jesus is the Plumb Line of 'Truth' by which the Father measured His Creation before it became defiled by sin. However, the story is not yet finished, God is working to see that all things are restored to the fullness of the standard of Christ, as all things will be summed up in Him at the end of the age.

    Ephesians 1:10 "...that in the dispensation of the fullness of the times He might gather together in one all things in Christ, both which are in heaven and which are on earth—in Him."

2. When we believe lies or entertain sin in our lives, we give the enemy a place in our world opening a door to our soul; the revelatory communication between God and ourselves is then <u>easily polluted and distorted</u>.

3. Patterns of thinking not aligned to the truth of God's Word can be the residue of our old unsanctified nature.

4. These patterns are a result of man's pride and will hinder in the apprehension of the whole counsel of God if not <u>cleansed by the Blood</u>.

5. The Life and Light of Jesus is <u>the filter that purifies</u> all teaching and doctrine. When surrendered to Him, Jesus will align our lives and our words with the Plumb Line of His Life to ensure they are the measure of His Standard.

6. He imparts the power for change when we choose Him, and through repentance and the cleansing our words and actions, <u>we become aligned</u> *with His*.

7. Jesus is the <u>Life source of everything</u> the Father has ever dreamed and purposed in creation. He is the Life and measure of the New Man the Father has been fashioning over the centuries, since the fall of Adam (1 Cor. 15:45-49).

8. Idolatry in the form of *self*-actualization—*self*-will, *self*-centeredness and *selfishness*—is presently widespread in the world today, also in the Body of Christ. God's first commandment addresses all such idolatry:

    Exodus 20:3: "You shall have no other gods before Me"

9. The only solution to iniquity is <u>repentance inspired by a return to the Cross</u>, and a fresh revelation of the awesome Christ in all His power and Glory!

10. It is imperative to our wellbeing that our eyes are fixed upon Jesus, beholding His *awesome* majesty and Glory. All that we teach, and practice must reflect the '*Lamb who was slain*' and point to the *resurrected Christ*.

___

Slide 24:

Ministry Time

Take some time to consider what are the influences that have worked to shape your present beliefs and worldview in either positive or negative ways, e.g. family, society, culture, the Bible or maybe Jesus?

Cleansing Prayer

Heavenly Father, LORD of all creation, please forgive me for exalting knowledge, philosophy, any scientific thought and any teaching or high thing that in my life has exalted itself above Your truth, Your Word and the knowledge of God. Forgive me for choosing disobedience to Your revealed Word.

I renounce *and break my agreement with every false way. I renounce and break agreement with all spiritual forces of wickedness and command them to go from my life to the LORD of hosts. I choose to embrace Your Living Word that teaches, corrects, exhorts and brings life to my soul. Your Word declares that humility and the fear of the LORD bring wealth and honor and life.*

Cleanse me *O Lord and realign all the thought patterns that are not in agreement with Your Word and establish me today on a new foundation. I plead the Blood of Jesus and ask that You apply it to every error and crooked way of thinking I have embraced in my life. Lord, I humble myself before you today.*

I declare *that You alone are the Fountain of Living water from which the Words of Life flow, imparting wisdom, understanding and healing to the humble soul. Thank You LORD! I now receive Your cleansing and healing touch.*

PRAYER OF SALVATION: If your desire is to come under this eternally secure protection, and you would like to become a member of God's family, simply open your hearts right now, turn your face towards heaven and pray this prayer in sincerity:

Father *in heaven, I believe You sent Your Son to die for me, to pay the penalty for my sin. I see that I am a sinner in need of the cleansing that comes only from the Blood of Jesus. Thank You for Your incredible Grace and mercy!*

Holy Spirit*, I invite you to come into my heart and be seated on the throne of my life. Guide my steps daily that I may walk rightly before You. Reveal to me your truth and give me wisdom and understanding of Spiritual and heavenly things.*

Jesus, *I invite you to be my Lord, to teach me Your ways that I may know You. Allow me to taste the Love that would give its life for me. Today I make my stand on Your side and choose you Jesus as my Lord and Savior. I now give You control of my life and surrender to You as my God and loving Savior. Amen*

SESSION II:
THE JOURNEY OF CLEANSING

Biblical Foundation

Slide 1: Romans 8:29 - "For whom He foreknew, He also predestined to be conformed to the image of His Son, that He might be <u>the Firstborn among many brethren</u>."

Root: conformed: *summorphos* - **FORMED IN UNION**

Slide 2:

THE BORN-AGAIN DYNAMIC

1. The destination of the <u>journey of sanctification</u> is fullness of union with Christ—a union that guarantees as an inheritance, all that is Christ and belongs to Christ. This only takes place under the <u>banner of His Lordship</u>!

    Acts 17:28 "...for in Him we live and move and have our being, as also some of your own poets have said, '<u>For we are also His offspring</u>.' Therefore, since we are the offspring of God, we ought not to think that the Divine Nature is like gold or silver or stone, something shaped by art and man's devising."

    1 John 4:9 "In this the love of God was manifested toward us, that God has sent His only begotten Son into the world, that <u>we might live through Him</u>."

2. God's purpose in the whole <u>plan of redemption</u> is that by the indwelling of the Holy Spirit, Christ is infused into the very matrix of man's being, permeating his spirit, soul and his thought processes until a Christ man *is produced*—this is a Christian.

3. *God* is not interested in men trying to attain to a standard like that of Christ to become somewhat like Him. His plan of redemption works to not only *'buy back'* man from his lost state but includes the possibility of conformity into the very image of Christ

4. The Greek word *summorphos* meaning to be <u>*formed in union*</u> as we said, illustrates the concept that as we are grafted *into His Body*, we are *becoming Christ*—our minds and hearts becoming united with His mind and His Heart.

Slide 3:

TRANSFORMED IN HIS LIKENESS

1. Jesus, the Holy One, chose to be born into our world in a dirty stable. Jesus dwells by the Holy Spirit in our spirit, however, I believe the stable can be a revelation of the condition of the <u>land of the soul at salvation.</u>

2. In this session we will use land, as an illustration, to portray the transformation of the soul in the <u>process of sanctification</u> There are countless illustrations in the Bible, drawing the analogy of *land* to our souls:

   Psalm 63:1 "Early will I seek You; My soul thirsts for You; <u>My flesh longs for You in a dry and thirsty land</u> where there is no water."

   Isaiah 44:3 "For I will pour water on him who is thirsty, and floods on the <u>dry ground</u>..."

_____

_____

_____

Slide 4:

TRANSFORMED IN HIS LIKENESS

1. Through redemption, the Holy Spirit occupies the <u>spirit of the man</u>, establishing a beachhead in his soul. However, the enemy may still occupy a significant place in the soul through old mindsets and strongholds of un-Godly beliefs.

2. The Lord has purchased the land with His blood and <u>owns it all</u>! This person is saved, forgiven and fully under the care, protection, and Lordship of Christ.

3. However, as the illustration shows, at salvation, even though we are given one hundred percent of the Lord, He does not necessarily receive <u>one hundred percent of us</u> at that time.

4. We enter a process where we are given the choice to continually surrender more of our lives to Him. To a certain degree, the soul may therefore be oppressed by the enemy who continually seeks entrance through <u>unguarded gates</u>.

   Deuteronomy 28:52 "They shall besiege you <u>at all your gates</u> until your high and fortified walls, <u>in which you trust</u>, come down throughout all your land which the Lord your God has given you."

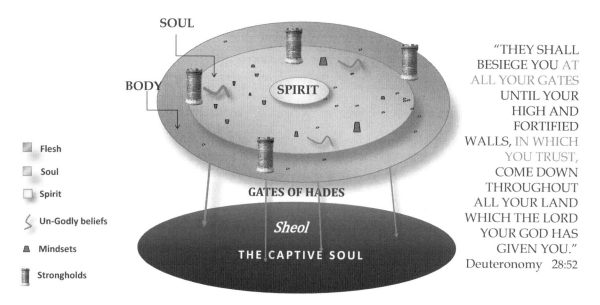

5. However, the land of this soul is completely under the rule of the Holy Spirit, who works through the spirit of man in the process of sanctification, to drive out the enemy and cleanse the land of iniquity.

6. We use the illustration in this diagram to portray the land of a person's soul who has become a Christian and, in whose spirit, the Holy Spirit has made His home and is in the process of being conformed in the image of Christ.

7. Because of sin, before we became Christians the soul was dominant, ruling over a very weak or sick spirit. God's intention is for the spirit of man to be the seat of His Throne from where He rules and reigns over the land of our soul.

___

Slide 5:

TRANSFORMED IN HIS LIKENESS:

1. The soul (mind, heart and will), was never designed to function in a place of authority and is not capable or equipped to lead and chart the course of man.

Proverbs 14:12 "There is a way that seems right to a man <u>but its end is the way of death</u>"

2. The soul, held captive by Satan through strongholds and mindsets, established due to personal or generational sin, or through trauma, keeps the spirit in <u>a place of captivity</u>, working to prevent it from rising and taking its place in ascendancy over the soul.

3. Let's look at the concept of illegal squatters. These are squatters who take up residence on land that has been abandoned, and not guarded or cared for. It could be land passed on through the generations that no one bothered to care for. However, God does have His purpose in this.

   Joshua 2:21-23 God said, "I will no longer drive out before them any of the nations Joshua left when he died. I will use them to test Israel and see whether they will keep the way of the Lord and walk in it as their ancestors did." The Lord had allowed those nations to remain; He did not drive them out at once by giving them into the hands of Joshua."

4. The land no longer belongs to the enemy. However, squatters do have rights under the law, and it can be exceedingly difficult to get rid of them. Sometimes you must go to court to get rid of them; if they have lived on the land for a certain length of time, they have legal rights.

5. These spiritual forces have become <u>illegal squatters</u> on our land and must be driven out and served an eviction notice.

Slide 6:

TRANSFORMED IN HIS LIKENESS

1. Because the soul does not have <u>the wisdom to rule,</u> Satan has been highly successful at invading our souls and establishing strongholds that are fortified and defended belief structures.

2. Demonic spirits work to keep the land in captivity, successfully restricting man's spirit from taking the place of ascendancy God intended it to occupy.

3. On the path of sanctification, God works to break through the pride, break down our wills, brings to death our old nature, delivers us from our enemies and bring us into the Glory of a life filled with all <u>the fullness of God</u>.

   Philippians 3:21 "...the Lord Jesus Christ, who, by the power that enables Him to bring everything under His control, will transform our lowly body that it may be <u>conformed to His glorious body, according to the working by which He is able even to subdue all things to Himself.</u>"

   _____
   _____
   _____

Slide 7:

TRANSFORMED IN HIS LIKENESS

1. The Holy Spirit works to break down our strongholds, change the patterns of our thinking, and transform the land from a wasteland into one that <u>flourishes and blossoms</u> with the life of Christ.

2. The Word teaches that we are responsible to guard our souls for what we believe and the course we take:

   Proverbs 25:28 "Whoever has no rule over his own spirit is like a city broken down without walls."

3. Through the work of sanctification, God leads us on the journey of faith that works to take us from one degree of <u>glory, faith, and strength</u> to another as the diagram shows. In this process, we are being completed in the Life of Christ.

   _____
   _____
   _____

Slide 8:

BEGINNING THE PATH OF SURRENDER

1. Sanctification is the term the Bible uses for the <u>journey of the Cross</u>, that transforms us in the way of the Cross as we are conformed to Christ.

Isaiah 40:4-5 "Prepare the way of the Lord; make straight in the desert a highway for our God. Every valley shall be exalted and every mountain and hill brought low; the <u>crooked place shall be made straight</u> and the rough places smooth; the glory of the LORD shall be revealed…"

2. Through this process our mountains and high places of pride must be brought to the Cross; our valleys of despair and unbelief must be raised up to the place of trust and faith, and the crooked places of un-Godly beliefs and error must be given over to the Lord.

3. On this journey with the Holy Spirit, there must be a <u>continual surrendering</u> and 'laying down' of one's own wisdom, agendas, ideas, thoughts, ambitions, possessions, family and '*works*.'

4. This is a process <u>we choose,</u> and must continually be saying, *"Yes Lord"* as He works deep within us, ploughing the soil of our 'land' and threshing the produce of our souls.

Slide 9:

BEGINNING THE PATH OF SURRENDER

1. As this diagram shows, the way of the Cross is a <u>clear and straight path</u> without any crooked areas of religion and deception, and the highs and lows of life are founded on unbelief and lack of trust in God.

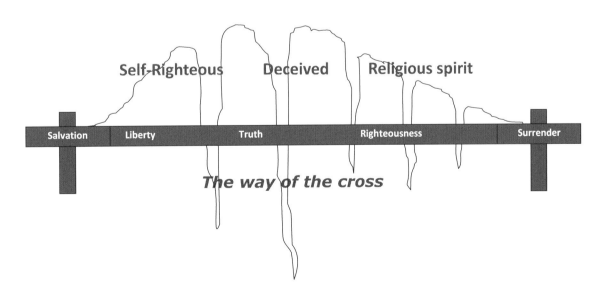

2. The way of the Cross is the way of sacrifice where we chose to present our bodies as living sacrifices acceptable to God.

   Romans 12:1 "Therefore, I urge you, brothers and sisters, in view of God's mercy, to <u>offer your bodies as a living sacrifice, holy and pleasing to God</u>—this is your true and proper worship."

3. When an electrocardiograph is showing a flat straight line, it signifies that the person is dead; in the same manner, the straight path of the Cross indicates death to the old nature and the <u>walk of a resurrected life</u> in Christ.

4. God's way for us to live a victorious life is not the way of the world, it is the Cross. It is a way of love, of yielding, where we give up our right for vengeance, to justify ourselves and for justice, where we trust the Lord to be our defense and our shield.

5. The way of the Cross leads us to walk daily within the <u>balance and tension</u> of the Mind and the Heart of Christ.

_____

_____

_____

Slide 10:

THE WAY OF THE CROSS – THE PATH TO GLORY

1. The entire process of sanctification takes place within the <u>context of death</u>, a spiritual concept that works continually to make way for the <u>resurrection life of Christ to arise</u> in us in our daily walk. It is death to <u>the person that we were,</u> as we rise in newness of life in resurrection Glory.

2. As the diagram shows, to travel the way of the Cross is a path of surrender—the goal in view to entering the <u>Sabbath rest of God</u>. It is the place where His yoke is easy, and His burden light, and He rises in us to accomplish His will.

   Galatians 2:20: "I have been crucified with Christ; it is no longer I who live, but Christ who lives in me…"

   Hebrews 4:10-11: "For he who has entered His rest has himself also ceased from his works as God did from His. Let us therefore be diligent to enter that rest…"

THE JOURNEY OF CLEANSING

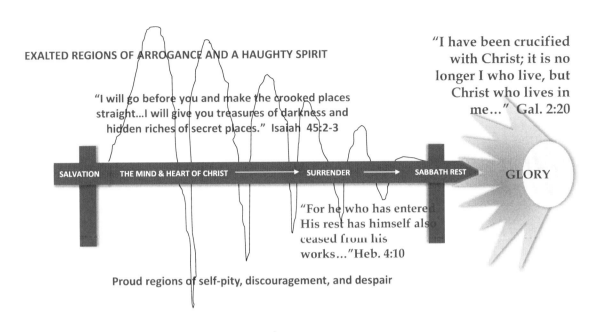

3. The way of the Cross is <u>the way of freedom</u> from the constraints of the world, the pull of sin, and the pride of life.

4. The journey of faith, from salvation to Glory, from pride to brokenness, from *'works'* to *'rest,'* is a journey that the Body of Christ and all servants of the Lord must travel to **Cross over** into Resurrection Power and Glory in the Promised Land of <u>our inheritance in God</u>.

Slide 11:

THE WORK OF THE CROSS

1. The way of the Cross is a straight path that leads to liberty, triumph over evil and resurrection life in the Promised Land of Christ. At the outset of the Journey God tells us:

   1 Peter 4:12: <u>"Beloved, do not think it strange concerning the fiery trial which is to try you,</u> as though some strange thing has happened to you..."

2. God's Power and strength m us at the Cross, we are then able through Him to defeat any foe. By choosing the Cross, God's incredible <u>providence is activated</u> in our lives and He can rule over every situation that we may encounter.

THE BRIDE MAKES HERSELF READY

3. The Holy Spirit works continually in the children of God to bring them into conformity to the image of Christ, especially those committed to serving Him in ministry. However, His ways of refining and training are tailored specifically to <u>the individual</u> in both timing and nature.

4. Throughout the trials and the testing on our walk with God, we are continually given an opportunity to choose the way that always leads to the release of abundant Life and the fulfillment of our destiny in Christ—*and that is the Cross.*

_____
_____
_____

Slide 12:

THE WORK OF THE CROSS

1. The journey of faith will take us through a series of crosses as we learn to embrace the Cross as a way of life. On this Journey God is continually at work in building our lives according to His blueprint:

    1. He works to perfect us <u>in Truth</u>
    2. Spiritual muscles <u>of faith</u> are being built in us
    3. Like Christ, we learn to <u>walk in obedience</u>
    4. We are strengthened to stand in the midst of adversity and <u>not be shaken by life.</u>
    5. We are shown our sin and brought to the place <u>where we hate sin</u>.
    6. We learn to overcome by walking through things that <u>we must overcome</u>
    7. We learn to war and are trained to be conquerors <u>in our battles</u>

_____
_____
_____

Slide 13:

THE WORK OF THE CROSS

1. **Continued:**

    8. The strongholds of fear are broken our lives <u>e.g. fear of failure, fear of man</u>

9. He brings us to dead ends where we are hedged in all around and the only door out is Jesus, we then learn to trust and rely on Him in all things
10. He is patient with us until we grow in maturity and learn to walk in His power and authority
11. He builds us together corporately as a Bride.
12. He establishes us that we may know and understand that we are sons and daughters of the Great King.

2. During this process, God builds many important and vital characteristics into our foundation that we may be able to possess the character and strength to walk in a manner worthy of His name.

Slide 14:

JESUS LIVED THE CROSS:

1. The significance of the Cross is revealed through Jesus' example by:

    1. His willingness to lay down His life in forgiveness & love for others (John 15:3)
    2. His willingness to choose only His Father's way (John 14:10)
    3. His willingness to give up His right for justice (1 Pet. 2:23, John 19:10-11)
    4. His willingness to give up His right for vengeance and retribution (John 18:10)
    5. His willingness to give up His right for compensation (Jn. 4:34 Matt. 5:46, 6:1)

Slide 15: THE WASTELAND BEGINS TO FLOURISH

1. God intends to transform the wasteland of our souls into a land that flourishes with the Life of Christ. He does this by pushing back the darkness, clearing the land of the strongholds erected by the enemy, and by filling it with His Presence and Glory.

THE BRIDE MAKES HERSELF READY

2. As the land flourishes under His care, transformation into the Promised Land of Christ takes place, where His throne becomes firmly established and receives <u>the rains of Heaven.</u>

THE PROMISED LAND OF THE SOUL

Deuteronomy 11:11: "But the land you are crossing the Jordan to take possession of is <u>a land of mountains and valleys that drinks rain from heaven.</u> It is a land the LORD your God cares for; the eyes of the LORD your God are continually on it from the beginning of the year to its end. So if you faithfully obey the commands I am giving you today—to love the LORD your God and to serve him with all your heart and with all your soul—then I will send rain on your land in its season, both autumn and spring rains, so that you may gather in your grain, new wine, and olive oil.

Slide 16: THE WASTELAND BEGINS TO FLOURISH

1. We are encouraged in the Word that Christ in us is the *hope of Glory*, and that when He appears, we will appear with Him in Glory (Col 1:27, Col. 3:4).

2 Corinthians 5:17 "Therefore, if anyone is in Christ, <u>he is a new creation;</u> old things have passed away; behold, all things have become new."

2. As the Kingdom of God becomes firmly established in the land of our soul, our Land is transformed into the promised land of Christ. We can then receive all the blessings rightfully ours as children of God as our land begins to bear big fruit!

3. When our lives are in order and aligned to the Plumb Line of Jesus' Life, the heavens are opened to us, <u>angels ascend and descend</u> upon God's purposes for our lives, and we are able to fully appropriate the fullness of our inheritance and blessings in Christ, in the heavenly places (Jn. 1:51, Gen. 28:12, Eph. 1:3).

4. The journey of faith demands that we lay down our lives in a continual and progressive surrendering of our wills to the will of God.

_____
_____
_____

Slide 17:

THE NEW CREATION

1. In the Last Days, the whole Creation will be set <u>free from the curse</u> and brought back to God's original intention (Isaiah 24:5-6).

2. It will travel through the Cross of Jesus Christ; it will be purged of iniquity and be resurrected as <u>a New Creation.</u>

    2 Peter 3:13 "Nevertheless we, according to His promise, <u>look for new heavens and a new earth</u> in which righteousness dwells."

_____
_____
_____

Slide 18: THE NEW CREATION

1. In this hour, the only safe place to live is under the shadow of the Cross, dwelling in <u>the secret place</u> of the Most High (Ps. 91).

THE BRIDE MAKES HERSELF READY

1 Thessalonians 5:23 - "Now may the God of peace Himself sanctify you completely; and may your whole spirit, soul and body be preserved blameless at the coming of the Lord Jesus. <u>He who calls you is faithful, who also will do it.</u>"

2. To live victorious lives, we must embrace the way of the Cross, the weapon that Jesus used to <u>defeat the enemy</u> and the only weapon that will continue to defeat him on our journey of faith.

_____
_____
_____

Slide 19:

THE LORD IS OMNICOMPETENT

1. **Our Lord is Omnicompetent**: He is able and <u>sufficient for all things</u>; nothing takes Him by surprise. He is faithful and He is prepared to handle every situation we face when all control is released to Him.

   Jude 24: "Now to Him who is <u>able to keep you from stumbling</u> and present you faultless before the presence of His Glory with exceeding joy."

   Philippians 1:6: "...being confident of this, that he who began a good work in you <u>will carry it on to completion</u> until the day of Christ Jesus."

_____
_____
_____

Slide 20:

OUR LORD IS OMNISCIENT

1. He perceives all things and has <u>complete knowledge</u>. His plan has been set in motion from the foundation of the Earth, it stands firm forever.

2. It is at work at this very moment and will continue to unfold until it <u>reaches completion.</u>

3. God's plan is so wide and so high, as a very small speck in its midst, we have not been able to see its fullness: but it does consider the completion of the work He begins in us at salvation.

   Psalm 94:10-15: "Does He who disciplines nations not punish? Does He who teaches mankind lack knowledge? The LORD knows all human plans; He knows that they are futile. Blessed is the one You discipline, LORD, the one You teach from your law; you grant them relief from days of trouble, till a pit is dug for the wicked. <u>For the LORD will not reject His people; He will never forsake His inheritance.</u> Judgment will again be founded on righteousness, and all the upright in heart will follow it."

Slide 21:

Ministry Time

Questions to consider: Would you agree that the principles of sanctification and cleansing are important to the process of becoming conformed to the image of Christ? If so, is this process actively at work in your daily experiences, conforming you to the image of Christ?

During a quiet time with the Lord, look for the places where you are resisting God in His work to conform you to Christ and to deliver you.

Seek the Lord for the areas where the enemy has a hold in your life, where you have been taken captive by him to do his will.

PRAYER OF SURRENDER

Heavenly Father, Holy and Omnipotent God, I come before You today with thanksgiving in my heart for having provided through Your Son Jesus, everything needed for my healing and deliverance, and for supplying the keys of freedom to live a Godly and righteous life that is holy and pleasing to You.

I Praise and worship You and lift up the Name of Jesus. Jesus, I acknowledge Your Lordship over my life today and surrender to the direction, control and power of the Holy Spirit through this process of deliverance. I love and welcome Your Presence Holy Spirit; I release all control over to You and yield my will to the way You choose to minister to me.

*Lord, I acknowledge according to Your Word in Colossians 2:15 that having disarmed all powers and authorities, Jesus triumphed over all the power of the enemy and made a public spectacle of him at the Cross. Lord Your incursion in into enemy territory was completely successful—You rescued me, brought me out and positioned me **in You,** in the Kingdom and family of God where the enemy has no authority to penetrate. I thank You for this Divine protection given through the Blood of Jesus that covers my life.*

Lord I acknowledge that it is Your Love that leads to repentance, that there is no condemnation for those who are in Christ; therefore, Lord I ask that you release a great manifestation of Your love to me today as we embark on this journey of cleansing and deliverance together. All this I ask in the Wonderful name of Jesus. Amen.

SESSION III:
HE HAS NOTHING IN ME

Biblical Foundation

Slide 1: "I will no longer talk much with you, for the ruler of this world is coming and <u>he has nothing in me</u>." John 14:30

Slide 2:

UNDERSTANDING THE LAW & FAITH

1. To understand the sphere of the enemy in our lives, we must first understand the place of <u>grace, law, and faith</u> in the lives of Christians. Jesus said that He was both the end and the fulfillment of the Law.

2. Jesus came to remove the hold of the law on His people through faith in His finished work on the Cross, and to release us to a life in union with *Him, <u>who fully kept the Law.</u>* We are now led, not by law, but by the Holy Spirit through faith.

    Romans 8:2-5 "...through Christ Jesus the law of the Spirit who gives life <u>has set you free from the law of sin and death.</u> For what the law was powerless to do because it was weakened by the flesh, God did by sending His own Son in the likeness of sinful flesh to be a sin offering. And so He condemned sin in the flesh, in order that the <u>righteous requirement of the law might be fully met in</u> us, who do not live according to the flesh but according to the Spirit."

Slide 3:

UNDERSTANDING THE LAW & FAITH

1. The righteousness of God is through faith! All are now <u>freely justified</u> by His Grace through faith!

2. Because Jesus gave His Life for us and took our punishment for sin, we have been released from the punishment of breaking the law when we lay claim by faith to <u>His atonement</u> for our sin.

Romans 3:20 "Therefore no one will be declared righteous in God's sight by the works of the law; rather, through the law we become conscious of our sin. But now apart from the law the righteousness of God has been made known, to which the Law and the Prophets testify. <u>This righteousness is given through faith in Jesus Christ to all who believe.</u> There is no difference between Jew and Gentile, for all have sinned and fall short of the glory of God, and all are justified freely by His grace through the redemption that came by Christ Jesus."

___
___
___

Slide 4:

UNDERSTANDING THE LAW & FAITH

1. Although we are no longer justified by the law, we were never given license to break the law—the law is holy, the <u>ten commandments</u> still apply to us. Jesus lived a life of faith that always honored the Word of God and those in union with Him will desire to do the same.

    Matthew 5:17 "Do not think that I have come to abolish the Law or the Prophets; I have <u>not come to abolish them but to fulfill them</u>. For truly I tell you, until heaven and earth disappear, not the smallest letter, not the least stroke of a pen, will by any means disappear from the Law <u>until everything is accomplished</u>."

2. The New Covenant in Christ, spoken of in the Old Testament and Quoted in the New, declares that the law was to be <u>written on our hearts</u>.

    Hebrews 8:10: "...I will put My laws in their mind and write them on their hearts, and I will be their God, and they shall be My people."

3. God's laws become a part of our hearts and minds we are being conformed to Christ! When we transgress and fall into sin, <u>grace gives us access to the Father</u> where we can repent and ask forgiveness. In the seven letters to the seven churches, Jesus says many times to repent.

___
___
___

Slide 5:

HAVE NO AGREEMENT WITH SIN

1. In the Courtroom of Heaven, Satan accused Job of serving God with ulterior motives. Today he does the same with all God's children, accusing us of sin and breaking the laws of God.

   Luke 22:31 "And the Lord said, "Simon, Simon! Indeed, Satan has asked for you, that he may sift you as wheat. But I have prayed for you, <u>that your faith should not fail</u>; and when you have returned to Me, strengthen your brethren."

2. Jesus did not say that He would deliver Peter, and stop Satan, but rather that He would pray for him that by faith <u>he would overcome</u> in the trial, in the same way, that Job overcame in his trial of faith.

3. Since we are now bought and paid for by the blood of Jesus, <u>the power of iniquity</u> has been broken. We can now come before God and petition Him for freedom from the reaping consequences of sin, based on the redemptive work of Christ on the Cross.

4. All bondages, oppression, hindrances, and restrictions placed in our way by the enemy, and legally applied because of iniquity, sin, and generational curses, can be nullified through repentance and holding fast to the <u>finished work of Christ.</u>

Slide 6:

HAVE NO AGREEMENT WITH SIN

1. Every Christian is engaged in a battle with the enemies of God, <u>in a war over their souls</u>. This is not a battle that we can see, as it is being fought in the spiritual realms, in the second heaven, from where these entities rule. Agreement with sin gives them a place in our souls.

   Ephesians 6:12-13 "For we do not wrestle against flesh and blood, but against principalities, against powers, against the rulers of the darkness of this age, against spiritual hosts of <u>wickedness in the heavenly places</u>. Therefore take up the whole armor of God, that you may be able to withstand in the evil day, and having done all, to stand."

Slide 7: HAVE NO AGREEMENT WITH SIN

1. The Word of God provides us with revelation and understanding of the underlying reasons many Christians give the enemy a place in their lives and the consequent problems they encounter.

   Isaiah 5:13-14 "Therefore my people have gone <u>into captivity</u>, <u>because they have no knowledge</u>, their honorable men are famished, and their multitude dried up with thirst. Therefore <u>Sheol has enlarged itself and opened its mouth beyond measure</u>."

2. Lack of knowledge and understanding of the spiritual impact of <u>personal or generational sin</u> in the life of the believer, gives place to complacency that allows the enemy free access to the lives of many, to steal, kill, and destroy (Jn. 10:10).

Slide 8:

DEMONIC OPPRESSION

1. Jesus was completely untainted by sin and the world. He fulfilled all the laws of God and was obedient unto death. He could therefore make the statement: "...*he has no hold over Me.*"

   NKJV – "...<u>nothing in</u> Me." NLT – "...no <u>power over</u> Me."

2. There was <u>nothing in Jesus</u> that the enemy could find that agreed with his principles, nature, or ways. As born-again believers, we also must be able to say with Jesus: "...*he has nothing in me.*"

   Proverbs 25:28 "Whoever has <u>no rule over his spirit</u> is like a city broken down, without walls."

3. In order to stand firm and not be shaken during the ever-increasing shaking the world will experience, these words must become <u>our truth and foundation</u>. It is to our detriment when we are complacent about sin, as it is an open invitation to demonic oppression.

Slide 9:

HAVE NO AGREEMENT WITH SIN

1. The Word of God admonishes us not to give the enemy a <u>foothold or place</u> in our lives by entertaining sin:

    Ephesians 4:27 *"Therefore, putting away lying, "Let each one of you speak truth with his neighbor," for we are members of one another. "Be angry, and do not sin": do not let the sun go down on your wrath, <u>nor give place to the devil</u>...Let no corrupt word proceed out of your mouth, but what is good for necessary edification, that it may impart grace to the hearers. And do not grieve the Holy Spirit of God, by whom you were sealed for the day of redemption. Let all bitterness, wrath, anger, clamor, and evil speaking be put away from you, with all malice. And be kind to one another, tenderhearted, forgiving one another, even as God in Christ forgave you."*

    The Greek word for *place* is *topos* and can also be defined as: *an opportunity, a home or a position of authority*

Slide 10:

HAVE NO AGREEMENT WITH SIN

1. We must therefore be careful not to give the enemy <u>an opportunity</u> because of sin or allow him to take up a position of authority that will have impact on our soul or our home. Jesus said that He would build His church, and the *"gates of Hades would not prevail"* against His people (Matt. 16:18).

    Prevail means: <u>to triumph, to win, overcome or be dominant.</u>

Slide 11:

DEMONIC OPPRESSION

1. Jesus has opened for us the way of access <u>to very throne of God</u>, where we are able to receive help, strength and sustenance in times of need.

    "Hebrews 4:14 "Seeing then that we have a great High Priest who has <u>passed through the heavens,</u> Jesus the Son of God, let us hold fast our confession."

    Hebrews 7:26 "Such a high priest truly meets our need—one who is holy, blameless, pure, set apart from sinners, <u>exalted above the heavens</u>."

___

___

___

Slide 12:

DEMONIC OPPRESSION

1. Jesus has triumphed over the forces of darkness; our sins are now forgiven and covered by His blood. Because of what Jesus did on the Cross we therefore fight, not for victory, but *from* <u>a place of victory.</u>

    Colossians 2:14-15 "...having wiped out the handwriting of requirements that was against us, which was contrary to us. And He has taken it out of the way, having nailed it to the cross. Having disarmed principalities and powers, <u>He made a public spectacle of them, triumphing over them in it</u>."

___

___

___

Slide 13:

DEMONIC OPPRESSION

1. We must understand that satan does have authority within the realm of sin and is a fanatical legalist. Whether consciously or unconsciously, we form a covenant of agreement with the enemy <u>because of our agreement with sin</u>!

THE JOURNEY OF CLEANSING

2 Timothy 2:25-26 "...if God perhaps will grant them repentance, so that they may know the truth, and that they may come to their senses and escape <u>the snare of the devil, having been taken captive by him to do his will.</u>"

2. Sin, and strongholds of un-Godly beliefs, give the enemy <u>a place in our hearts</u> and our world; they attract demons bent on mischief and trouble—oppressive diabolical entities who share our space.

3. As a consequence of sin, the enemy then gains a platform on which to stand and accuse; a breach occurs in our defenses; *Sheol, another name for Hades* opens her mouth and a 'gate' is opened through which the soul is taken captive by the enemy to harass, oppress and steal every good thing God has intended for us.

4. Deuteronomy 28 spells out clearly God's <u>condemnation of sin</u> and the consequences of disobedience to His Word; it also reveals the unbelievable blessings for obedience and a walk of righteousness before God.

5. It is important to stop here to clarify that God's intentions were never to restrict us and place us in bondage to religious laws because of a desire to control us. God intends to provide us with incredible freedom from all strongholds and bondages the enemy lures us into by providing <u>safe boundaries</u> in broad open places, where we live an abundant life in the freedom of mind, body, and soul.

_____

_____

_____

Slide 14:

DEMONIC OPPRESSION

1. Sin allows <u>demonic activity</u> in the land of our soul, and therefore in the heavens over our land, producing a mixture in our lives and our Christian walk, and pollution in the revelatory stream between God and man, as you see illustrated in the diagram.

2. In the same manner that dirty water will attract flies and bacteria, when we drink from broken cisterns—<u>the lies of the enemy</u>—we attract the forces of hell through sin and rebellion.

3. Our communion with the Lord, then greatly hindered, also becomes susceptible to defilement, as shown.

THE BRIDE MAKES HERSELF READY

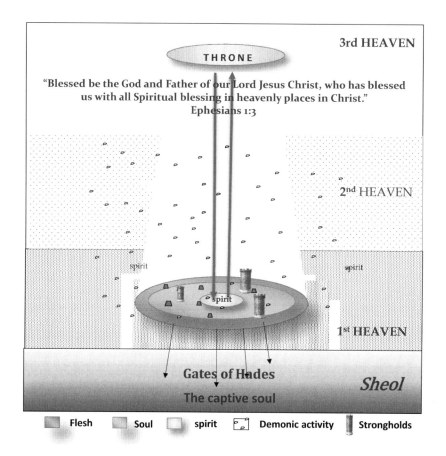

4. Even though the sun is always shining, clouds can come before it and block its rays of light; in the same way, demonic oppression caused by sin, <u>forms a cloud of darkness</u> between us and the light of the Lord.

5. When there is oppression it can be difficult to perceive His voice and His Presence, even though He has never left us, and never will when our heart is turned toward Him.

___

Slide 15: DEMONIC OPPRESSION

1. The enemy lays traps for <u>the unsuspecting</u> when they make bad choices and are then taken captive to prisons of oppression, despair an,d hopelessness, which can lead to anger and unbelief.

THE JOURNEY OF CLEANSING

Colossians 2:8 "See to it that no one <u>takes you captive through hollow and deceptive philosophy</u>, which depends on human tradition and the basic principles of this world rather than on Christ." NIV

Acts 8:23 "For I see that you are <u>full of bitterness and captive to sin</u>."

___
___
___

Slide 16:

UNDERSTANDING DELIVERANCE:

1. The enemy can hold the soul captive and keep it bound to time, people, and places <u>where sin has occurred</u>, and to spiritual regions where there has been great trauma. However, God says:

   Psalm 86:13 "For great is Your mercy toward me, and You have delivered my soul from <u>the depths of Sheol</u>"

2. When we repent and apply the blood of Jesus to our sin, the power of the cords that have <u>kept us bound</u> to people, places, and dark regions can then be broken.

3. We can then seek the Lord for the cleansing of our souls, the defiled land and places of our sin, and the restoration of our souls to wholeness.

___
___
___

Slide 17: UNDERSTANDING DELIVERANCE

1. It is critical to understand that in the areas where God grants deliverance, that we are to fill that place with <u>the Lordship of Christ.</u>

2. Complacency in faithfully <u>maintaining our deliverance</u> in submission to God, will attract forces seven times greater as Jesus stated:

   Matthew 12:43-45 "When an unclean spirit goes out of a man, he goes through dry places, seeking rest, and finds none. Then he says, 'I will return to my house from which I came.' And when he comes, he finds it empty, swept, and put in order. <u>Then he goes and takes with him seven other spirits more wicked than himself, and they enter and dwell there; and the last state of that man is worse than the first."</u>

3. A vacuum will always be filled <u>with something!</u> To remain free the vacuum must be filled with the Lordship of Christ. He is deserving of nothing less.

___

Slide 18: LIVING UNDER OPENED HEAVENS:

1. As we cooperate with the Lord, He begins to work with us in the process of clearing the land of its idols, demolishing the strongholds, and removing the high places, the enemy's hold is broken, our souls are released from captivity, the darkness clears, and the <u>heavens open over our lives</u> as shown in the diagram.

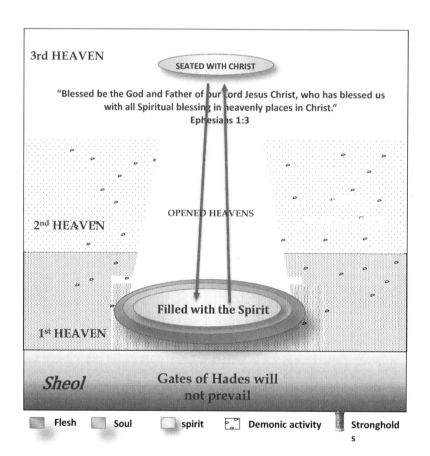

2. We can then receive all the blessings rightfully ours as children of God, as the Kingdom of God becomes firmly established in our soul, we are filled with the Holy Spirit and become the Promised Land of God.

3. As we grow up and rise into the stature of Christ, the gates of Hades no longer have power or legal right in our lives, and we are not shaken by their attempts to destroy us.

4. We then gain free access to the blessings that are rightfully ours as children of God as they begin to flow freely into our lives. The Kingdom of God then becomes firmly established in our lives as we are continually filled with the Holy Spirit and He begins to occupy more territory in us.

Slide 19: LIVING UNDER OPENED HEAVENS:

1. In our past lives as unbelievers, we walked in covenant with satan through agreement with his ways and principles; our minds were blinded, set according to the flesh, and covered by a veil of deception.

2. Our hearts were hardened and darkened, our thoughts futile, and we were clothed in garments of unrighteousness—our father was the father of lies and we bore his image to some degree (2 Cor. 3:14, Rom. 1:21).

3. When our lives become aligned to the Plumb line of Jesus' life, we receive the gift of being filled with the Holy Spirit without measure, the heavens are opened to us, angels ascend and descend upon God's purposes for our lives, and we can fully appropriate the fullness of our inheritance and blessings in Christ as sons of God (Jn. 1:51, Gen. 28:12, Eph. 1:3).

   2 Corinthians 10:5-6 "We demolish arguments and every pretension that sets itself up against the knowledge of God, and we take captive every thought to make it obedient to Christ. And we will be ready to punish every act of disobedience, once your obedience is complete."

4. We can then fully appropriate the fullness of our inheritance and blessings in Christ in the heavenly places when our obedience is complete.

Slide 20:

CONFORMED TO A NEW IMAGE:

1. In the process of becoming 'sons of God,' when our *'obedience is complete,'* God works to remove every trace of Satan's image from us and re-fashions us in the image of Christ in glory (Rom. 8:29).

   2 Corinthians 3:18 "But we all, with unveiled face, beholding as in a mirror the glory of the Lord, are being transformed into the same image from glory to glory, just as by the Spirit of the Lord."

2. God will remove all our filthy rags and clothe us in His royal garments of praise and righteousness.

Slide 21:

CONFORMED TO A NEW IMAGE

1. Transformation takes place within the context of repentance. Whether corporately or individually, God requires that His people humble themselves in true humility and repentance. He desires that we break away from habitual sin, to receive forgiveness and deliverance in the land of our souls.

2. When we truly humble ourselves before the Father, we can corporately cry out to Him to heal our cities and nations and our prayers will ascend before the throne of God like incense.

   Chronicles 7:14 "If My people who are called by My name will humble themselves, and pray and seek My face, and turn from their wicked ways, then I will hear from heaven, and will forgive their sin and heal their land."

2. A deep change of heart is necessary to produce the fruit of repentance—like an overused antibiotic we can become dull to the effects of the Word of God if we simply mimic these words.

3. Through spending time in God's Presence, we become sensitive to His Spirit, and more aware when we grieve Him through sin, a wrong attitude or maybe a harsh word to someone.

Slide 22:

CONFORMED TO A NEW IMAGE

1. If we are willing, the Lord will walk with us through a time of <u>deep repentance and cleansing</u>, and by His awesome power the enemy's hold will be broken and we are set free:

   Isaiah 1:19 "If you are willing and obedient, <u>you will eat the best from the Land</u>" NIV

2. Cleansing of body, soul, and spirit, allows us to walk in <u>Kingdom realities</u>, in the atmosphere of heaven as ambassadors of Christ to a fallen world.

3. As the world descends into the darkness of the last days, it is so important and vital to our safety and the safety of our families that we can say in Christ, *"...he has nothing in me."* The light of Christ that we reflect must be <u>bright, strong, and pure</u>.

   Isaiah 60:1-2 "Arise, shine; <u>for your light has come!</u> And the glory of the Lord is risen upon you. For behold, darkness shall cover the earth, and deep darkness the people; but the Lord will arise over you, and His glory will be seen upon you."

4. The principles of sanctification, cleansing, and deliverance are all important parts to the process of becoming conformed to the image of Christ?

Slide 23:
Ministry Time

What are the places where you are resisting God in His work to conform you to Christ and to deliver you from bondage to sin?

Seek the Lord for the areas where the enemy has a hold in your life, where you have been taken captive by him to do his will.

Cleansing Prayer

Heavenly Father, I confess that because of sin in my life I have given legal right to the enemy to oppress me and steal the good things You have promised me in Your word. I confess that I have compromised on Your word and have not been diligent to obey You and follow Your ways. Please forgive me for coming into agreement with the enemy of my soul. Forgive me Lord for stubbornness, pride and rebellion. Forgive me giving the destroyer an opportunity or an open door to take my soul captive and cause me pain and sorrow.

Lord, I renounce *the works of darkness and choose today to break every covenant and place of agreement between myself and the Kingdom of darkness. I repent for holding on to unforgiveness in my heart and choose today to release forgiveness to_____*

Cleanse me *Lord and wash me from every trace of defilement by the enemy and bring the land of my soul under the protection of the Blood of Jesus.*

I declare *that all legal rights the enemy has used against me have been nailed to the Cross where Jesus triumphed and was victorious over Satan. Now in Your authority and by the Blood, I cancel and declare them invalid. I break the power of sin in my life and all ties to the time and the land of my sin. By Your finished work on the Cross, I now break the power of any curse against me and cancel all assignments of evil by the precious Blood. Lord I now commit myself to Your care and Lordship over my life. I thank you that in Christ I am forgiven, Bless Your holy name!*

MODULE II:
DELIVERANCE & RELEASE

SESSION 1:
FORCES HINDERING RELEASE

Biblical Foundation

Slide 1: "*I am* He who lives, and was dead, and behold, I am alive forevermore. Amen. And I have the <u>keys of Hades and of Death</u>."

Slide 2:

HOLDING THE GROUND

1. In the process of deliverance, the question that God takes into consideration is whether *His* children have the character and strength <u>to hold the ground that He has destined for them</u>?

2. The reason for this is the especially important spiritual principle Jesus taught in Luke 11:24-26, that always works to destroy any gains that are made. God will therefore delay our deliverance as we grow in maturity to become strong in faith, obedient to His Word, and submitted to the Lordship of Christ. We can also see this principle in Joshua 2:21-23:

   "**I will no longer drive out before them any of the nations Joshua left when he died. <u>I will use them to test Israel and see whether they will keep the way of the LORD</u> and walk in it as their ancestors did." The LORD had allowed those nations to remain; he <u>did not drive them out at once</u> by giving them into the hands of Joshua.**"

3. So, God sometimes holds back our release, until we have <u>grown in maturity</u> in Christ to overcome the forces that work aggressively to undermine our progress.

4. The Lord waits until our spiritual <u>capacity increases</u> and our faith and trust in God grows to a level where we can stand and <u>hold the ground</u>, He so longs to give us.

Slide 3:

HOLDING THE GROUND

1. The Holy Spirit, therefore, works to conform us to the <u>mind and heart of Christ</u>, that we may walk in His ways and become a vessel prepared and equipped to pour out His love and compassion on humanity.

THE BRIDE MAKES HERSELF READY

2. We will succeed on the journey of sanctification when we become intentional about <u>obedience to the Word of God</u>, His principles, and His ways.

3. In 2 Timothy Paul instructs Timothy in the importance of <u>maintaining a clean heart</u> and a walk of righteousness, important to occupying and holding ground.

2 Timothy 2:21-25 "If you keep yourself pure, you will be a special utensil for honorable use. Your life will be clean, and you will be ready for the Master to use you for every good work. Run from anything that stimulates youthful lusts. Instead, pursue righteous living, faithfulness, love, and peace. Enjoy the companionship of those who call on the Lord with pure hearts. Again, I say, don't get involved in foolish, ignorant arguments that only start fights. A servant of the Lord must not quarrel but must be kind to everyone, be able to teach, and be patient with difficult people. NLT

_____

_____

_____

Slide 4:

HOLDING THE GROUND

1. As the Land of our souls becomes <u>cleared of its idols</u>, we must hold the ground that we have gained as we will find ourselves continually going around the mountain again and again.

2. In light of this, it becomes very important that we understand what the <u>root causes</u> are that are hindering the process and our advancement—*the reasons that we continually lose the ground we gain.*

3. Let us look at a few of the root causes that will continue to hinder us:

1. **Not aligned** <u>to the Plumb Line of Christ</u> – His mind & ways

2. **Agreement with satan** – ungodly beliefs, <u>not rightly dividing the Word</u>

3. **Pride & arrogance** – <u>God honors humility</u>

   Psalm 131:3 "<u>My heart is not proud, LORD</u>, my eyes are not haughty; I do not concern myself with great matters or things too wonderful (profound) for me.

Slide 5:

HOLDING THE GROUND

4. **Pride & Arrogance continued**

1. Let us continue to look at the issue of pride and God's desire for humility, as it is the <u>only avenue</u> to attaining the fullness and blessings of God.

   Psalm 149:4 "For the LORD takes delight in His people; He crowns the humble with victory."

   Isaiah 66:2 "These are the ones I look on with favor: those who are humble and contrite in spirit, and who tremble at My word."

   2 Chronicles 36:12: "He did evil in the eyes of the LORD his God and did not humble himself before Jeremiah the prophet, who spoke the word of the LORD."

2. This very significant scripture reveals the need to <u>honor leaders who serve God</u>, sent to us by God, for our benefit and our wellbeing.

Slide 6:

HOLDING THE GROUND

4. **Pride & Arrogance continued**

   To be spiritually mature means:

   - We are not opinionated: <u>obstinate or conceited concerning the merit of one's own opinions; conceitedly dogmatic.</u>

   - We recognize we do not know or understand everything

   - We recognize we only have part <u>of the picture</u>

- We understand our position and our boundaries – that we are not God
- We do not function under an Absalom spirit, stirring <u>others against leaders and gather them unto oneself</u>

Slide 7:
HOLDING THE GROUND

5. **False expectations** equal disappointment: <u>We need to let go of some things in order to move forward!</u>

6. **Divided heart** – Who or what is on the throne of your heart! <u>God searches for those who are wholehearted; vessels of gold fit for the master's use (Read: Phil. 3:8-15, 2 Tim. 2:20)</u>

    Galatians 2:20: "I have been crucified with Christ; <u>it is no longer I who live</u>, but Christ lives in me; and the *life* which I now live in the flesh I live by faith in the Son of God, who loved me and gave Himself for me.

7. **Shallow foundations** – <u>not being grounded in the Word of God</u>

8. **Not secured in the love & faithfulness of God** – God word to us is, <u>*"Never doubt Me!"*</u> Like David, we are bound securely in the Godhead:

    1 Samuel 25:29 "…but the soul of my lord shall be bound in the bundle of life with the LORD thy God…"

    This means to be secured within the <u>Godly boundaries of God's family,</u> through love, submission, accountability, honor, cooperation, and contribution that is the fruit of <u>humility.</u>

Slide 8:
HOLDING THE GROUND

9. **Fear & unbelief:** James says that unbelief is sin and if we live in unbelief, we will not <u>receive the promises.</u>

James 1:6-8 "But let him <u>ask in faith, with no doubting</u>, for he who doubts is like a wave of the sea driven and tossed by the wind. <u>For let not that man suppose that he will receive anything from the Lord</u>; he is a double-minded man, unstable in all his ways."

Slide 9:

HOLDING THE GROUND

10. **Fear of Death:**

    The people of God have no reason to fear death as we have eternal <u>security in Christ</u>. Whether life or death we are in a win, win situation.

    Revelation 1:17-18 "And when I saw Him, I fell at His feet as dead. But He laid His right hand on me, saying to me, "Do not be afraid; I am the First and the Last. I *am* He who lives, and was dead, and behold, I am alive forevermore. Amen. <u>And I have the keys of Hades and of Death.</u>"

Slide 10:

HOLDING THE GROUND

11. **Fear of Death continued**

    Acts 21:13 "Then Paul answered, "What do you mean by weeping and breaking my heart? For I am ready not only to be bound, <u>but also to die at Jerusalem for the name of the Lord Jesus.</u>"

THE BRIDE MAKES HERSELF READY

Slide 11:

HOLDING THE GROUND

12. **Fear of the enemy:** The enemy <u>fears Christ</u> and Christ dwells in power in each of us!

    Numbers 14:9 "Only do not rebel against the LORD, nor fear the people of the land, <u>for they *are* our bread</u>; their protection has departed from them, and the LORD *is* with us. Do not fear them."

    Psalm 27:1 "The LORD *is* my light and my salvation; <u>whom shall I fear</u>? The LORD *is* the strength of my life; of whom shall I be afraid?"

    Psalm 27:5 "For in the time of trouble He shall hide me in His pavilion; In the secret place of His tabernacle He shall hide me; He shall set me high upon a rock. God *is* <u>our refuge and strength, A very present help in trouble</u>."

Slide 12:

HOLDING THE GROUND

13. **Fear of Man** – the fear of man will rob the people of God of the great destiny God has prepared for us. We must fight to overcome this fear as we press forward on the path God has set before us. As we move out in faith, we will find that <u>fear disappears.</u>

    Hebrews 13:6 – "So we may boldly say: "The Lord is my helper; I will not fear what can man do to me?"

Slide 13:

HOLDING THE GROUND

14. **Fear of Risk & Fear of Mistakes:** When our eyes are fixed on Jesus, like Peter, we will be able to walk on water. Fear of mistakes is rooted <u>in an orphan spirit</u>, from which we need deliverance. God is our faithful Father, he has not left us <u>as orphans</u> to fend for ourselves.

2 Timothy 1:7 – "For God has not given us a spirit of fear (timidity), but of power and of love and of a sound mind.

Psalm 56:3 – "Whenever I am afraid, I will trust in You."

Slide 14:

HOLDING THE GROUND

15. **Fear of God:** A healthy fear of God that is <u>a reverence and awe</u> of His majesty, great power, and His glory, keeps us safe and humble before Him. As His word says, *on this one He will look.*

    Luke 12:4 "And I say to you, my friends, do not be afraid of those who kill the body, and after that have no more that they can do. But I will show you whom you should fear: Fear Him who, after He has killed, has power to cast into hell; <u>yes, I say to you, fear Him!</u>"

    Job 28:28: "And to man He said, 'Behold, <u>the fear of the Lord, that *is* wisdom</u>, and to depart from evil *is* understanding."

Slide 15:

WHAT IS YOUR SPIRITUAL PERSPECTIVE?

1. As we grow in maturity in Christ our spiritual perspective changes. We leave the earthly realm and begin to <u>ascend into the heavenly realms</u> to take our place seated at the right hand of God in Christ.

2. It is a journey of ascending and breaking through into <u>third heaven realities</u>. We are in control of the timing of our journey by your obedience and by choosing our perspective and taking our position.

THE BRIDE MAKES HERSELF READY

3. We will look at three positions we can assume and their consequent perspective, on the journey of the ascent to the Throne. The first is:

CAUGHT IN THE WHIRLWIND

- **Perspective is subjective** – <u>slanted, biased, one-sided</u>
- Eyes are on the circumstances
- Caught in the trap by emotions
- Placing excessive emphasis on one's own moods, attitudes, opinions
- Moved by justice & revenge
- Pleading, begging prayer – without faith

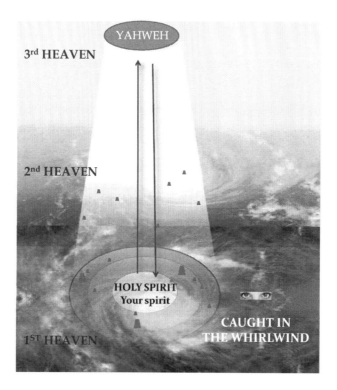

PERSPECTIVE: SUBJECTIVE

_____
_____
_____

Slide 16:

ACHIEVING ASCENDANCY

- **Perspective objective:** <u>not influenced by personal feelings, interpretations, or prejudice; unbiased</u>
- Beginning to rise above circumstances
- Emotions are submitted to God
- Moved by a clearer understanding of situations by revelation
- Overcoming sin in our lives
- Tearing down Strongholds – and old mind-sets
- Demolishing high things – opinions exalted above God
- Beginning to pray with confidence & faith

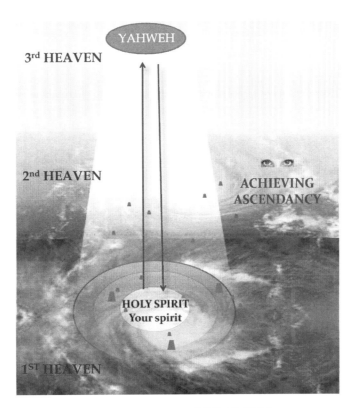

PERSPECTIVE: OBJECTIVE

Slide 17: SEATED AT THE RIGHT HAND

Hebrews 12:2: "Looking unto Jesus, the Author and Finisher of *our* faith, who for the joy that was set before Him endured the cross, despising the shame, and has sat down <u>at the right hand of the throne of God.</u>"

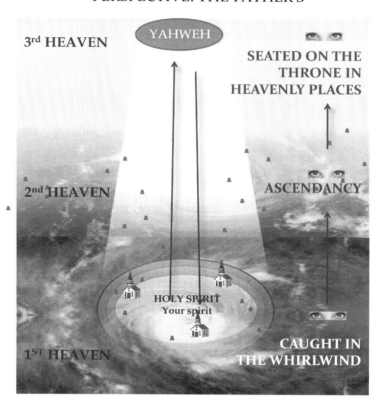

- **Perspective** – <u>The Father's</u>
- Eyes fixed on God
- Clear discernment
- Liberty through knowledge of Truth
- Moved by *Christ's* compassion & mercy
- Authority in prayer and the intercession of the overcomer
- Governmental Authority to Decree, Bind & Loose
- Legislating the Heavens with Christ
- The enemy is under our feet
- The Church is established
- Angels are in attendance
- We win the battles
- When the enemy has laid siege – We Ascend!
- WE ARE HEIRS OF GOD! NO LONGER SLAVES!

Slide 18:

MOVING FORWARD THROUGH REPENTANCE

1. **By keeping the right perspective – let us learn to ascend.** God has given us two keys to keep us moving forward and ascending. These are Repentance and forgiveness. Let us look first at God's plan in repentance.

2. Moving forward with strength in the excellence of the Spirit begins with repentance! John the Baptist went ahead to prepare the way for Jesus with a baptism of repentance.

3. As John preached a message of repentance in preparation for Christ's coming, the message of repentance shall again be heralded in preparation of His return.

    Matthew 3:2: "Repent, for the kingdom of heaven is at hand!"

4. Cleansing of body, soul and spirit through repentance allows us to walk in the fullness of Kingdom realities.

5. As the world descends into the darkness of the last days, it is so important and vital to our safety and the safety of our families that we can say in Christ, *"...he has nothing in me."* The light of Christ that we reflect must be bright, strong, and pure.

Slide 19:

MOVING FORWARD THROUGH REPENTANCE

1. We must return and remove by repentance everything that agrees with the enemy, this, in order inter into full union with the mind and heart of Christ and do great exploits in His name.

    Mark 1:15 "The time is fulfilled, and the kingdom of God is at hand. Repent, and believe in the gospel."

2. To believe in the Gospel is to believe in the fullness of the Gospel of Jesus Christ and all the treasure that is embedded within it—<u>the signs, the wonders, the power and the Glory.</u>

    Revelation 3:18 "I counsel you to buy from Me gold refined in the fire, that you may be rich; and white garments, that you may be clothed, *that* the shame of your nakedness may not be revealed; and anoint your eyes with eye salve, that you may see. As many as I love, I rebuke and chasten. <u>Therefore be zealous and repent</u>."

3. Bill Johnson: *"Most Christians have repented enough to get forgiven, but not enough <u>to see the Kingdom.</u>"*

Slide 20:

MOVING FORWARD THROUGH FORGIVENESS

1. Through the act of Jesus' forgiveness, 'Forgiven' became the Father's declaration over all humanity; He said*:*

    Luke 23-34 "Father forgive them, for they do not know what they do."

    John 3:16-17 "For God so loved the world that He gave His only begotten Son, that whoever believes in Him should not perish but have everlasting life. For God did not send His Son into the world to condemn the world, but that <u>the world through Him might be saved.</u>"

2. The power of the Father's forgiveness given through Christ, gives the world the possibility of release from the grip of sin, and removal from the condemnation and judgment it <u>presently dwells under</u> (Is. 24).

3. However, freedom and salvation come only with the recognition of <u>one's need for forgiveness</u>, acknowledging the finished work of Christ, and receiving Him as Savior.

CLEANSING THE BLOODLINE I

Slide 21:

MOVING FORWARD THROUGH FORGIVENESS

1. The power in the act of receiving or giving forgiveness <u>brings liberation</u> from bondage to sin, releases healing to our bodies from sickness and disease, and liberty from torment to our minds.

   John 20:23 "If you forgive anyone his sins, they are forgiven; if you do not forgive them, they are not forgiven."

2. Forgiveness removes the <u>control element</u> that has kept everything bound up, releasing the Lord to heal our hearts, and the freedom to begin His work in the other person's life.

_____

_____

_____

Slide 22:

MOVING FORWARD THROUGH FORGIVENESS

1. The Father requires our obedience to forgive others just as he has forgiven us in His Son. He is looking for sons and daughters who are conformed to the character and nature of Jesus, willing to be <u>big enough in spirit to forgive</u>.

   Matthew 6:15 "For if you forgive men when they sin against you, your heavenly Father will also forgive you. <u>But if you do not forgive men their sins, your Father will not forgive your sins</u>."

2. By allowing unforgiveness to find a home in our hearts, our souls are kept in a state of torment and captivity, making a way for diseases to <u>attack our bodies</u>.

3. Without releasing forgiveness, we will not receive the healing and deliverance we are longing for, and the liberty to walk in the power, in the fullness of our inheritance in Christ (Matt. 18:33-34).

_____

_____

_____

SLIDE 23:

MOVING FORWARD THROUGH FORGIVENESS

1. Forgiveness is not only for our benefit and well-being but also for the benefit of the <u>Body of Christ</u>, as every act of forgiveness releases the resurrection Life of Christ into the Body, bringing it into greater health, wholeness, maturity, and union.

2. Mature sons and daughters live from the <u>fruit of forgiveness</u> and receive their inheritance in Christ.

   2 Corinthians 2:11 "And what I have forgiven—if there was anything to forgive—I have forgiven in the sight of Christ for your sake, in order that Satan might not outwit us. <u>For we are not unaware of his schemes</u>."

3. Forgiveness is also for Jesus' sake as it wins for Him the reward of <u>His sacrifice</u>. Selah.

_____
_____
_____

Slide 24: THRONE UNION

1. As we ascend on this journey, we are not only given access to the Throne, we have been given <u>a place at the Throne of God</u>, where we have authority to rule in partnership with Him.

   Zechariah 3:4-6: The angel said to those who were standing before him, "Take off his filthy clothes." Then he said to Joshua, "See, I have taken away your sin, and I will put fine garments on you." Then I said, "Put a clean turban on his head." So they put a clean turban on his head and clothed him, while the angel of the LORD stood by. The angel of the LORD gave this charge to Joshua: "This is what the LORD Almighty says: 'If you will walk in obedience to me and keep my requirements, then you will <u>govern my house and have charge of my courts, and I will give you a place among these standing here.</u>

2. Let us press on to <u>the place of ascendancy</u>, to the Throne where we can unite with Christ and the Father for His will to be done on Earth as it is in Heaven.

_____
_____
_____

SESSION II:
CLEANSING THE BLOODLINE I

Biblical Foundation

Slide 1: Numbers 14:18 "The Lord is longsuffering and abundant in mercy, forgiving iniquity and transgression; but He by no means clears the guilty, visiting the iniquity of the fathers on the children to the third and fourth generations."

Slide 2:

GENERATIONAL SIN

1. <u>Access to the bloodline</u> and the DNA of humanity was secured by the serpent when in rebellion, Adam and Eve ate of the tree of the knowledge of good and evil, in disobedience to God's command.

2. The bloodline of man became polluted by iniquity through their <u>choice to disobey</u>. Rebellion and hatred against God's ways consequently found its place in the heart of man and the disease of pride spread into the heart of mankind.

3. Through disobedience and rebellion to His Word, the <u>curse on iniquity</u> travels down to all future generations, and the justice and the love of God demanded that all sin be cursed. The two principles of <u>blessings and cursing</u> can therefore be at work in our lives, passed on from our ancestors of previous generations.

    Exodus 20:5-6 "...you shall not bow down to them or serve them. For I the Lord your God, am a jealous God, <u>visiting the iniquity of the fathers upon the children to the third and fourth generations</u> of those who hate Me, but <u>showing mercy to thousands to those who love Me and keep My commandments</u>."

4. Yes, as born-again believers, <u>all our past sins are forgiven</u>, however, the enemy can still hold a place in our lives through:

    - The strongholds, mindsets and ways inherited from our ancestors
    - Sinful patterns established in our souls over the course of our lives
    - Present sin and rebellion.

1. The good news is that through Christ, God has given us the authority and the power through <u>His Name and His blood</u>, to remove through repentance, any stronghold and everything not aligned to His ways.

Slide 3:

GENERATIONAL SIN

1. Generational iniquity is passed on to the children in two ways:

    1. **Generational Curses:** The first claims made on the land of our souls, are therefore made <u>at conception</u>, by spirits legally functioning under the generational curses on the sins of our ancestors. These curses can cause familial inherited genetic defects.

        2 Samuel 12:9 "Why have you despised the commandment of the LORD, to do evil in His sight? You have killed Uriah the Hittite with the sword; you have taken his wife *to be* your wife, and have killed him with the sword of the people of Ammon. <u>Now therefore, the sword shall never depart from your house…</u>"

        Because of David's sin, his son died in childbirth and many disasters in his life and his family's life followed.

    2. **Generational traits:** These are traits in attitude, ways and personality acquired through <u>family and close relations</u>. These are ways that produce and promote a bent toward sin and iniquity. Let's first look at what could be a generational trait.

Slide 4:

GENERATIONAL TRAITS

1. We each have ways that are peculiar to us, and <u>very different from God's ways</u>—ways that may be peculiar to our family line.

    The Greek word for 'way' is *derek*, defined as: <u>*a road, figuratively a course or mode of action.*</u>

CLEANSING THE BLOODLINE I

MOSES ASKED: Exodus 33:13 "Now therefore, I pray, if I have found grace in Your sight <u>show me now Your way</u>, that I may know You and that I may find grace in Your sight."

Slide 5:

GENERATIONAL TRAITS

1. Generational ways or traits in personality manifest through the <u>interrelationships</u> of families affecting the way we relate to others.

   Psalm 39:1 "I said, I will guard my ways, lest I sin with my tongue…"

2. These traits can be inherent in the <u>genetic make-up of families</u> through curses or are simply acquired through close association over time, for example, addictive personalities, a bent toward a certain mindset, or certain character flaws such as stubbornness, anger or fear.

   Isaiah 55:8-9 "My ways are not your ways,"

3. God declared that His ways are much higher than our ways. We all have ways that may not appear terribly sinful to us; however, if our ways do not line up with the plumb line of God's ways, it may hinder <u>the revelation of God's Glory</u> in our lives.

Slide 6:

GENERATIONAL TRAITS

1. These are some negative generational ways evident in families that will affect our relationships with others and with the Lord.

   1. *Controlling* – <u>moved to continually tell others what to do, demanding that your way is the right way</u>
   2. *Aggressive* – <u>an aggressive manner in relating to others that breeds intimidation</u>

3. *Self-centred* – the conversation is always centered around you, you are always on your mind
4. *Domineering* - monopolizing the conversations, know it all attitude, not preferring others
5. *Angry* – very easily set off, people have to walk carefully around you
6. *Arrogant or dogmatic* – close-minded to other points of view
7. *Proud* – boastful, always having to be one up on others
8. *Argumentative* – contentious, defensive, eager to argue and debate
9. *Superior* – spiritually superior attitude toward others
10. *Manipulative* – using deceitful ways to get one's own way
11. *Fearful* – timid about change and new things
12. *Procrastination* – leaving things to the last minute, never on time
13. *Negative*: complaining. murmuring, grumbling and finding fault
14. *Loud and abrasive* – speaking too loudly and prone to interrupting constantly

_____

_____

_____

Slide 7:

GENERATIONAL TRAITS

1. These ways can be a source of contention in relationships between husband and wife, between parents and children and between friends.

2. Humility is required to begin to *see our ways* that are not beneficial in establishing enduring relationships.

   Psalm 95:10 "For forty years I was grieved with that generation, and said, "It is a people who go astray in their hearts, and they do not know My ways."

3. Believers are all God's workmanship and as we press into Him and seek His Face, He will shed light on the personality traits causing us problems in our relationships with others.

4. We come to know God in the secret intimate times we spend with Him. In this place, we learn of *His ways*, we are convicted of sin and are changed and transformed in His Presence.

5. Through spending time with the Lord, we will become like Him, conformed to His character and ways.

   Micah 6:8 "He has showed you, O man, what is good. And what does the LORD require of you? <u>To act justly and to love mercy and to walk humbly with your God.</u>"

Slide 8: GENERATIONAL CURSES

1. We are all fashioned in iniquity, and ultimately responsible for our own lives, <u>*despite our family's history.*</u> We must all persevere in overcoming sin and choose to wrestle through our own battles to become victorious.

   Psalm 51:5 "Surely I was sinful at birth, sinful from the time my mother conceived me. <u>Surely you desire truth in the inner parts</u>; you teach me wisdom in the inmost place." NIV

2. God spoke into existence specific curses on sin <u>as a deterrent</u> to pursuing a sinful life apart from Him (Deut. 28-30). Generational curses are passed on in the family line because of man's continual disobedience to God's ordinances and precepts.

3. One example of a generational pattern of iniquity is revealed in the lives of Abraham and his son Isaac; both involved their wives <u>in deception</u> about their marital status to save themselves, *at the expense of their wives' safety* (Gen 12:10-13, 26:6-9).

4. Generational curses administered by demonic spirits have the legal right to function in families through <u>generational iniquity not repented of</u> or cleansed by the blood of Jesus.

5. The evidence of generational curses in operation can be clearly seen operating in families having within their history certain <u>outstanding patterns</u> such as alcoholism, all forms of abuse, child abuse, financial difficulty, violence, bizarre accidents and premature deaths, sexual sin, hereditary diseases, Masonic curses, anti-Semitic curses, addictions, and occult curses.

Slide 9:

GENERATIONAL CURSES

1. After Gideon was drafted as the leader of God's army, and before he could safely go to war, his first assignment from the Lord was to tear down his father's altars and idols and build an altar to the Lord!

    Judges 6:25-26 "Take your father's young bull... and tear down the altar of Baal that your father has, and cut down the wooden image that is beside it; and build an altar to the Lord your God on top of this rock..."

2. All written requirements against us were nailed to the Cross in Christ at His crucifixion (Col. 2:14). The Blood of the Son of God became the atonement for our sin; cleansing and deliverance from the oppression of generational curses and spirits is, therefore, possible for all!

3. Identificational repentance for our sin and the sins of our forefathers, as in the example of Daniel's prayer, allows us to appropriate the Blood of Jesus and releases God to remove the generational curse and set us free (Dan. 9:4).

_____

_____

_____

Slide 10:

GENERATIONAL CURSES

1. Generational sin requires repentance for the curse to be broken. Judgment came upon Jerusalem in a certain instance because of the curses they had inherited from their forefathers in a previous generation:

    Jeremiah 15:4 "I will hand them over to trouble, to all kingdoms of the earth, because of Manasseh the son of Hezekiah, king of Judah, for what he did in Jerusalem.

2. Israel has been given to us as an example. The debt owed was carried forward to a future generation. The debt for sin must be paid; if the Blood—the price Jesus paid for the debt of sin is not applied, the curse is in operation and we inherit the debt.

3. All generational ties that hinder the Army of God must be broken before we engage in the great battles ahead, we must tear down our father's altars by repentance and allow God to cleanse us by the Blood.

CLEANSING THE BLOODLINE I

Slide 11:

GENERATIONAL CURSES

1. The breaking of generational curses over our lives is not a formula; usually, certain requirements need to be fulfilled before the Lord breaks the power of the curse, such as:

    ➢ <u>Sufficient recognition</u> and understanding of the generational sin, the hold it has on us, and how it is presently affecting our lives.

    ➢ <u>Sufficient qualitative repentance</u> for the place given over to the sin.

    ➢ <u>The timing of God</u>—when God is satisfied that we have grown with the character to be able to *hold and occupy* the ground He gives; He will break the yoke of the enemy.

2. God does sometimes begin a work in a person by breaking a curse, but usually, He takes His time building <u>His character</u> in us before deliverance comes— *as the result of breaking a curse prematurely could be seven times worse* according to Matthew 12:45.

Slide 12:

GENERATIONAL CURSES

1. The principle of timing is reflected in various accounts in Scripture. In the parable of the wheat and tares, Jesus taught that the tares sown by the enemy would grow to fullness, together with the wheat, <u>until harvest time</u> at the end of the age—at this point the evil tares are then gathered and burned.

    Matthew 13:40-41 "The harvest is the end of the age, and the harvesters are angels. As the weeds are pulled up and burned in the fire, so it will be at the end of the age. The Son of Man will send out his angels, <u>and they will weed out of his kingdom everything that causes sin and all who do evil.</u>

THE BRIDE MAKES HERSELF READY

_____

_____

_____

Slide 13:

DARK PRACTICES

1. God created mankind with a deep longing for a <u>relationship with Him</u>. He gave us a physical body, but also a spirit that yearns for connection with its maker, one that has the ability to communicate and respond spirit to Spirit and is sensitive to activity in the spiritual realm.

2. This becomes a significant problem for seekers of truth, as there are malevolent forces in these realms who desire to take unto themselves the worship that rightfully <u>belongs to God</u>.

3. These evil beings intend to lure, deceive and ensnare and they are also able to disguise themselves as <u>angels of light</u>.

    Deuteronomy 18:9-13 "When you come into the land which the LORD your God is giving you, you shall not learn to follow the abominations of those nations. There shall not be found among you anyone who makes his son or his daughter pass through the fire, or one who practices witchcraft, or a soothsayer, or one who interprets omens, or a sorcerer, or one who conjures spells, or a medium, or a spiritist, or one who calls up the dead. <u>For all who do these things are an abomination to the LORD,</u> and because of these abominations the LORD your God drives them out from before you. You shall be blameless before the LORD your God."

_____

_____

_____

Slide 14   DARK PRACTICES

1. God's prescribed way for man to receive revelation is only through a relationship developed in prayer and communion with the Father and given through the Holy Spirit at His discretion—not on demand.

    Leviticus 20:6 "And the person who turns to mediums and familiar spirits, to prostitute himself with them, I will set My face against that person and cut him off

from his people. Consecrate yourselves therefore, and be holy, for I am the LORD your God."

2. **The occult is defined as** *any system claiming use or knowledge of secret or supernatural powers or agencies; beyond the range of ordinary knowledge or understanding; mysterious, secret; disclosed or communicated only to the initiated; hidden from view.* Two such systems are divination and sorcery.

3. *Divination*: Any practice that seeks supernatural information through any source other than God such as, astrology and séances.

4. *Sorcery* - Another form of the occult, is the practice of persons who exercise supernatural powers through the aid of evil spirits, and witchcraft; the intent is to control others through spells, curses, incantations, hexes, hypnosis, black magic or any other form of mind-control.

Slide 15:

THE OCCULT

1. Other known practices having a demonic foundation: Ouija board, I Ching, Astrology and horoscopes, Wicca, palm reading, Tarot cards, some Aromatherapy, certain essential oils, even perfumes e.g. Sexual, Poison, etc., Seances, Kabbalah, Alchemy, Rosicrucianism and the Illuminati.

2. All involvement in satanically inspired occult practices or any spiritual activity that gives worship to Satan is expressly forbidden by God and will open doors to the demonic and lead to oppression.

3. This generation has inherited many curses from our ancestors but there are certain ones so diabolic and deeply rooted, where satan receives open and direct worship, that they lead to severe oppression and sometimes require ongoing deliverance. Chief among these are Masonic, occult curses.

Slide 16:

FREEMASONRY

1. The Masonic lodge is a men's organization that is a <u>secret society</u>. Each degree of its thirty-three degrees requires an initiation that is comprised of rituals that include the taking of demonic oaths.

2. In reality, this is a covenant of agreement with <u>the dark side</u>.

   Isaiah 28:15 "You boast, "We have entered into a covenant with death, with the grave we have made an agreement. When an overwhelming scourge sweeps by, it cannot touch us, for we have made a lie our refuge and falsehood our hiding place."

3. Many unsuspecting men, including Christian men, become members of the Masonic Lodge without having any understanding of its <u>occult foundations</u>.

4. Each Degree and Rite has its own set of rituals, oaths, regalia, handshake, ceremonial clothing, symbols, and tools that in some way either give worship or exalt the powers of darkness. In the Bible, God calls these things <u>an abomination</u>.

_____

_____

_____

Slide 17:

FREEMASONRY

1. These oaths <u>are an agreement</u> where the initiated willingly agrees to declare curses of sickness, great harm, pain, torture, and even death on themselves and their families as a consequence of any disclosure of the secrets of the Lodge.

2. The Word of God discourages the taking of vows or oaths. When we take an oath, it causes us to become <u>locked into a *covenant of agreement*</u> that we are bound to keep because of the honor of our word (James 5:12).

3. God takes the making and breaking of covenants very seriously! When King Saul broke the covenant, Joshua had made with the Gibeonites, even though Joshua was wrong to do it, God was terribly angry and called for a three-year famine on the land (2 Samuel 21:1).

Numbers 30:2 "If a man makes a vow to the LORD, or swears an oath to bind himself by some agreement, <u>he shall not break his word; he shall do according to all that proceeds out of his mouth</u>."

4. The Masonic Lodge worships and <u>embraces all gods</u>. The 33rd degree gives entrance to the level of the Shriners, a group that has many benevolent causes, however, part of the initiation for entrance into the Shriners is swearing on the Koran and dedication to the Islamic faith with reference to Allah as the God of our fathers.

5. The fuel supplying the stronghold of the Masonic Lodge comes through Leviathan the god of pride, and Jezebel who introduced the children of God to the worship of Baal and Ashtoreth.

6. Jezebel did this under the cover and protection of her husband Ahab, an Israelite King. Today, these spirits continue to work under the covering and protection of churches where the leadership <u>embraces membership to the Lodge</u>.

Slide 18:

FREEMASONRY

1. The contract Masons have made with *Sheol* is <u>binding and is to be honored</u>, and the penalty for breaking it must be paid. The only avenue of escape is to make an appeal to a higher court based on Colossians 2:13-15.

   "**When you were dead in your sins and in the uncircumcision of your sinful nature, God made you alive with Christ. <u>He forgave us all our sins, having canceled the written code, with its regulations, that was against us and that stood opposed to us;</u> he took it away, nailing it to the cross. And having disarmed the powers and authorities, he made a public spectacle of them, triumphing over them by the cross.**" NIV

2. Jesus paid the penalty to break the covenant with Death and Hades. He declared in Matthew 16:18 that the gates of Hades would not and could not <u>prevail over His people.</u>

3. The word prevail means *to prove superior in power, strength or influence*. Jesus broke the contract with *Sheol* and the enemy's power when He allowed Himself to become the scapegoat <u>on whom all the punishment was laid</u>.

4. All curses spoken by Masons over themselves and their families, <u>Jesus took the penalty</u> upon Himself on the Cross. As children belonging to God, we can now make our appeal to the Great Judge of the universe, based on the finished work of Jesus, by His Blood that was shed.

5. We can break the power of the agreement, <u>nullify every contract and claim</u> made, and with authority cancel all possible repercussions. We have the authority to charge the enemy with fraud for attempting to collect on a contract previously paid and have him bound and sent to prison.

___

Slide 19:

CULTIC RELIGIONS

1. Any and every religion that does not give Jesus His place as God and Savior, that gives veneration to any person, image or ideal other than Christ, is cultic.

2. Cultic religions are easily identified, as the foundation of their religion is based on one of five premises:

   1) The worship of idols: <u>*anything* other than the Father, Son, and Holy Spirit</u>

   2) The belief that we can appease God <u>through a system of rituals, works or tradition.</u>

   3) The belief that humans are gods, or that through a system of rituals and practices can <u>become gods outside of Christ</u>.

   4) The worship of a plethora of gods and goddesses <u>with an attempt to commune with them</u>

   5) The <u>spiritual control</u> and domination of one charismatic, authoritarian leader over the direction of the lives and finances of the people he leads.

Slide 20:

CLEANSING THE HOUSE

1. In this age of civilization, the mystery of iniquity continues its <u>ravenous path</u>, as sin escalates toward fullness and completeness in the earth.

2. The depravity of humanity runs deep through thousands of years of iniquity and has been present in the Father's House for four thousand years (since Abraham).

3. It continues today as Christians choose <u>to embrace the world</u> and the things of the world.

    2 Kings 23:24 "Moreover Josiah put away those who consulted mediums and spiritists, the household gods and idols, all the abominations that were seen in the land of Judah and in Jerusalem, that he might perform the words of the law which were written in the book that Hilkiah the priest found in the house of the LORD."

Slide 21:

CLEANSING THE HOUSE

1. In the House of God, the fullness of time is upon us for the restoration of all things.

2. In preparation, the Father is releasing His angels to cleanse and <u>gather out from His House all things that offend Him,</u> remove all curses from His people and set them free!

    Matthew 13:40-41 "Therefore as the tares are gathered and burned in the fire, so it will be at the end of this age. The Son of Man will send out His angels, and they will gather out of His kingdom all things that offend, and those who practice lawlessness..."

Slide 22:

Ministry Time:

Reflect on your family line, are there any outstanding traits, sinful tendencies, diseases or addictions that are evident and deeply rooted? These are a few negative generational ways evident in families that may be affecting our relationships with others, with the Lord, and consequently, hinder our walk in Christ:

Cleansing Prayer

Most Holy Father, I stand before You today in humility, I come by the way of the Blood of Your Son to seek your mercy. I ask Your forgiveness for myself and my forefathers, for our sin and rebellion to Your ways. We have not wholeheartedly obeyed Your commands and Your precepts and Word. We have trampled on the Holy Spirit's heart time and time again. Lord, I don't deserve Your mercy but You are Good and Your mercy endures forever. Lord, I ask Your forgiveness and choose today to turn away from all sin.

I now renounce and break agreement with all generational sin and traits, I renounce the sinful ways of my ancestors and my sin/s of _____, I now make a deliberate choice to walk in Your Ways as You strengthen me.

Cleanse me Lord from sin by Your great power, and in Your mercy, break the power of iniquity that runs through the generations of my family and place the precious Blood of Your Son who died for my sins, on all the gates of my life. Seal my spirit with the Blood and be the Wall of fire that forever guards and preserves my life for Your Glory.

I declare that You alone are the Lord of my life, You are the Rock on which I make my stand, You alone will I serve all the days of my life with your strength and faith rising up in me daily. May my life be a praise to Your name and shine for the glory of Your Son that He may receive all the honor, praise, and Glory due His great name. I love You Lord, Have Your Way.

Jesus is now taking off the garment of sin and shame, He is putting on you His Royal robes of Love, Joy, Acceptance and Life on you!

SESSION III:
CLEANSING THE BLOODLINE II

Biblical Foundation

Slide 1: Colossians 1:16 "For by Him all things were created that are in heaven and that are on earth, visible and invisible, whether thrones or dominions or principalities or powers. All things were created through Him and for Him." Colossians 1:16

Slide 2

THE IMAGE OF SATAN

1. Jezebel and Leviathan are <u>satanic spirits</u> in the kingdom of darkness, that reign as powers over the earth, infecting humanity with their sinful nature of pride, arrogance, control and sexual pervasion.

2. They are busy at work in Governments, leaders, education, media, science and the entertainment industry.

3. They are also busy at work within the Church <u>attempting to control it</u> and infect it thereby preventing its destiny from coming forth—*but God is seated on His Throne!*

   Colossians 2:15 "Having disarmed principalities and powers, He made a public spectacle of them, <u>triumphing over them in it</u>."

Slide 3

THE IMAGE OF SATAN

1. We are admonished in Scripture to ask God to search our hearts for any <u>wicked way</u> that may be hidden from our eyes.

   Psalm 139:23 "Search me, O God, and know my heart: try me, and know my thoughts: And see if *there be any* wicked way in me, and lead me in the way everlasting."

THE BRIDE MAKES HERSELF READY

2. As we examine the nature of Jezebel and Leviathan let us ask God to shine the Light of Christ in our hearts to expose any <u>area of agreement</u> with these anti-Christ powers.

_____

_____

_____

Slide 4

THE IMAGE OF SATAN

1. The spirits of Leviathan and Jezebel are spirits representing the characteristics of the nature of Satan.

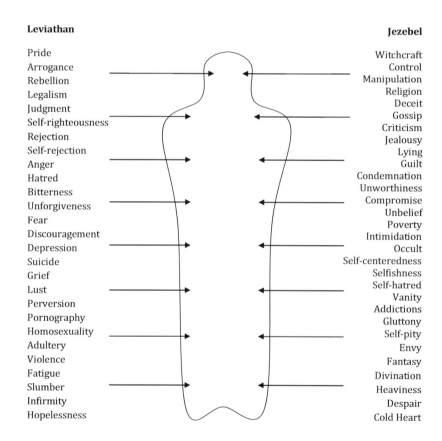

2. These powers <u>bear the image of Satan</u>, and their nature has been deeply entrenched in family bloodlines, through agreement with sin. This has caused much of the world to reflect their characteristics.

3. The lists in the diagram are not meant to be stereotypes of men and women as Leviathan and Jezebel both depict <u>the essence of the devil</u>. These spirits do oppress both men and women, and both genders are having to deal with many of these issues.

Slide 5

RECOGNIZING JEZEBEL

1. Jezebels seeks to destroy the <u>prophetic word of God</u>, given through the prophetic gift, a gift necessary for the building up and edification of the House of God.

   1 Kings 18:4 "For it was *so*, <u>when Jezebel cut off the prophets of the LORD</u>, that Obadiah took an hundred prophets, and hid them by fifty in a cave, and fed them with bread and water." KJV

2. This spirit's present attempt to do this is by polluting and <u>contaminating the prophetic</u> stream with demonic influences, given the right to oppress because of sin.

Slide 6

RECOGNIZING JEZEBEL

1. Defilement in the prophetic <u>produces confusion</u>, misunderstanding and misinterpretation of God's intention and direction through the prophetic word (Rev. 2:20).

2. Jezebel's agenda is always <u>to control</u> as this hinders the moving of the Holy Spirit and stifles freedom and liberty. Control is the agenda behind all witchcraft.

   Revelation 2:20 "Nevertheless I have a few things against you, because you allow that woman Jezebel, who calls herself a prophetess, to teach and seduce My servants to commit sexual immorality and eat things sacrificed to idols."

THE BRIDE MAKES HERSELF READY

3. This spirit controls through, domination, intimidation, and manipulation. The methods sometimes used are anger, threats, fear, criticism, sexuality and lust, slander, gossip, flattery, belittling, sulking, self-pity, and even sometimes tears.

___

Slide 7 JEZEBEL'S NATURE

1. **Rebellious** – rebels against the laws of God, the ways of God and His methods used to accomplish His purposes. God will use only *His means* to accomplish His end, *"For rebellion is as the seed of witchcraft, and stubbornness is as iniquity and idolatry"* (1 Sam. 15:23).

2. **Proud** – blind to one's own sin, self-centered, <u>wise in own eyes, arrogant and haughty.</u>

3. **Independent of God** – does things its own way, <u>arrogant, un-submitted to God's established authority in any form.</u>

4. **Stubborn** – refuses to change, to yield, and to bow; <u>continues in the same patterns even after there is recognition of sin.</u>

5. **Religious** – Is legalistic and set in ways of doing things and patterns of thinking; <u>refuses to yield (Jam. 3:17).</u>

6. **Deceitful** – Intent on getting one's own way, shifts blame, <u>wants to look good at all costs to the extent of hurting others (1 Sam. 15:13-26).</u>

7. **Jealous** – likes to put others down, <u>does not like to see others succeed.</u>

8. **Vicious** – can become violent in a rage

___

Slide 8 JEZEBEL SUCCESSFULLY WORKS THROUGH

1. <u>**Through Corporate & Church leaders**</u> – Jezebel intends to bring division in the Body of Christ through misuse of power, spiritual abuse, offense, a sharp tongue, immorality,

compromise, fear, criticism, control, unforgiveness, the putting down and non-recognition of women.

These all work to create a breeding ground for the Jezebel spirit to function freely.

2. **The congregation** – Criticism and judgments of leadership, criticism and judgments of each other, seeking ways to control and manipulate leadership, seeking ways to control others, gossip, offense and unforgiveness. Jezebel has been successfully infiltrating churches that don't hold to the standard of the Word of God.

3. **The Family** – Hostility between husband and wife, manipulation, domination and control, seduction and abuse, withholding sex, deception, criticism; rebellion by children inspired from parents ruling without love.

4. **Seduction** – Jezebel will release sexual spirits of adultery, lust, perversion, homosexuality, pornography and masturbation to destroy the man or woman of God and the Church of God.

Slide 9

RECOGNIZING LEVIATHAN

Traits inspired by the spirit of Leviathan:

1. **Independent:** argumentative, contentious, strong in own strength, will not ask for help from others.

2. **A hard or cold heart:** speaks harshly and aggressively, does not cry as it is a sign of weakness, a walled city, hard to penetrate protective walls.

3. **Stubborn:** cannot admit wrong, cannot say sorry, set in ways, will not yield.

4. **Perfectionist:** overly concerned with appearances, exalts physical beauty, given to jealousy and rage, loves position, boastful.

5. **Slumbering spirit:** There may be sleepiness when praying, reading the Word or hearing an anointed message (*not always a result of this spirit*).

Slide 10

LEVIATHAN'S NATURE:

Psalm 74:14 "You broke the heads of Leviathan in pieces."

1. **Proud** – arrogant *"He beholds every high thing; he is king over all the children of pride."* Job 41:34

2. **Ruler** – Authoritarian, dictatorial, rules by law rather than by love through relationship

3. **Religious** – Denominational pride, divisive, dogmatic, unyielding, inflexible, stubborn, stiff-necked

4. **Self-worship** – self-centered, self-importance, self-exaltation, self-righteous, given to self-promotion

Slide 11

TARGET OF LEVIATHAN:

Jezebel and Leviathan will oppress both men and women, but as Jezebel tends to target women, Leviathan tends to target men.

1. **Communication:** A distorter of communication: **distort**: to make crooked, **distortion**: *a change in the form of a signal during transmission, impairment of quality, distort the appearance and misrepresent* (motives, facts and statements).

2. **Leadership:** Leviathan targets leadership in all areas of society e.g. Government and politics, the Church, businesses, and organizations. Leads or rules with intimidation desires power and attempts to take God's place and role in the Church.

3. **Men:** This spirit's strategy is to prevent men's ministries from being birthed altogether or to render them ineffective and fruitless, without purpose.

- This spirit becomes most dangerous when the enemy takes possession of the leadership of a men's ministry, group, or organization and it becomes a force, an army or a cult for the purposes of Satan, e.g. Masons, Nation of Islam, Neo Nazi groups and many others.

- This spirit seeks through men to also belittle, demean, and trivialize women and women's ministries. Its purpose is to keep women enslaved.

Slide 12 TARGETS OF LEVIATHAN

1. **Women** – This spirit intends to keep women in captivity, to prevent the full revelation of the purpose of God for women from coming forth. Women who are affected by Leviathan will appear to manifest the masculine qualities of leviathan such as a tough hard exterior, strong in own strength, despises weakness and tears.

2. **Marriages** – Leviathan operates in marriages in both husbands and wives wherever pride is at work. More than any other time in history God is releasing husbands and wives together in ministry as a team as He did Pricilla and Aquila.

    There is a revelation coming forth, of the scope of the blessing that God intends for the husband and wife in agreement and truly one that the enemy wants to keep hidden.

3. **Worship & Music** – The enemy recognizes that worship and praise are weapons against him and will therefore target people in this ministry. This spirit seeks either to minimize the importance of worship or to shift the focus from the Lord to the leader.

    True worship, holy and undefiled cannot flow through pride. This spirit tries to bring division to the team through offense, anger, and jealousy.

4. **Finances** – Deceives through pride in the ability to create and control mammon, pride in self-sufficiency; is against any outside control over finances, e.g. God through tithing and offerings. Must retain control over finances.

Slide 13

BATTLING LEVIATHAN

1. **Francis Frangipane:** *"There is a difference between repenting for a sin and actually pulling down the <u>stronghold within us that produces the sin</u>. The first involves faith in the Cross of Christ; the second demands we embrace the crucifixion ourselves. This is the essence of pulling down strongholds: we destroy the defiling, oppressive system of thinking which, through the years, has been built into our nature."*

2. Pride is the greatest battle we will ever fight, as it is <u>deeply entrenched</u> within humanity inherited at the fall. The spirit of pride is a stronghold that is firmly established in the soul of mankind where it wages war against us.

3. Pride is extremely deceptive and can hide under many <u>layers of consciousness</u>. It takes God to reveal it. It will disguise itself with attributes of moral excellence and benevolence and good works.

4. However, pride does not escape the eye of God that lays bare the soul and detects every motivation of the heart. Both Leviathan and Jezebel represent the <u>King of pride</u> himself – *satan*

_____
_____
_____

Slide 14

BATTLING LEVIATHAN

1. There is only one way to win the battle over pride and remove its influence from our lives and that is by humbling one's self before God and embracing the Cross of His Son that defeated it. *<u>Pride cannot fight pride.</u>*

2. Some important things to consider in our warfare against Leviathan the king of pride according to the book of Job:

   - **<u>Do not be presumptuous:</u>** *"If you lay your hand on it, you will never forget the battle that follows, and you will never try it again!"* Job 41:8

   - **<u>Impossible to overcome him in our own strength</u>**: *"Indeed any hope of overcoming him is false...No one is so fierce that he would dare stir him up."* Verses 9-10

- **With his armor of pride, he is proud of his ability to withstand attack:** *"Who can remove his outer coat." Verse 13*

- **It is difficult to penetrate his defenses as he hides within so many layers:** *"His rows of scales are his pride, shut up tightly as with a seal" Verses 15-16.*

- **He shields himself with other demons** e.g. rejection, self-righteousness, shame, fear, and religious spirits; these are all demons associated with a stronghold of pride: *"one is so near another that no air can come between them; they are joined one to another, they stick together and cannot be parted" Verse 17*

Slide 15

BATTLING LEVIATHAN

1. God created Leviathan and only God can remove or destroy him:

   Psalm 104:26 "See the ships sailing along and Leviathan, <u>which You made</u> to play in the sea."

   Isaiah 27:1 "In that day the LORD with His severe sword, great and strong will punish Leviathan the fleeing serpent, Leviathan that twisted serpent; <u>He will slay the dragon that is in the sea.</u>"

Slide 16

HEALING & DELIVERANCE

1. Humility is a prerequisite <u>for deliverance</u>! The Word of God says to humble ourselves under the mighty hand of God and He will exalt us in His time. It also says that God resists the proud and gives grace to the humble.

   1 Peter 5:5-6 "God opposes the proud but shows favor to the humble. <u>Humble</u>

THE BRIDE MAKES HERSELF READY

yourselves, therefore, under God's mighty hand, that he may lift you up in due time."

2. In the atmosphere of humility, we can receive revelation and understanding of the areas in our lives that need God's work.

3. The insecurities in man will allow the spirit of pride to inspire us to be proud *even of our humility*.

___

Slide 17

HEALING & DELIVERANCE

1. There can be a variety of spirits at work oppressing an individual—from mild to severe oppression. If you find that in praying into a particular area, you begin to experience sudden sharp pains, nausea, extreme coughing, choking or any strange behavior, it is best to seek your leaders for advice.

2. Deliverance can sometimes be an instantaneous event but often, it is a very slow process where God works to break down our strong wills and our great pride.

3. During this process, our eyes are opened, and we begin to understand the level of the sin nature within us and we become intentional about becoming free.

4. This builds within us a foundation to be able to hold the ground of our deliverance and grow in maturity.

   Hebrews 10:35-37 "So do not throw away your confidence; it will be richly rewarded. You need to persevere so that when you have done the will of God, you will receive what he has promised. For, "In just a little while, he who is coming will come and will not delay."

5. When God is satisfied with our response and sees that we can hold the ground that He gives, without falling back into old ways (Matt. 12:43-45), *that day will be the day of our deliverance.*

SESSION IV:
REPROGRAMMING THE BRAIN

Biblical Foundation

Slide 1: Romans 7:23 "For in my inner being I delight in God's law; but I see another law at work in me, waging war against the law of my mind and making me a prisoner of the law of sin at work within me."

Slide 2:

REPROGRAMMING THE BRAIN

1. Let us now look at the ways of escape and freedom God has provided for us from the <u>pull of iniquity</u>. Beginning with our brains. The brain will both work for us and against us.

2. The processes of the brain—intended by the creator to serve us for our good, will ultimately work against us to <u>derail God's work</u> of deliverance if we are not diligent to protect the ground we have taken and our new walk in the spirit.

3. Our beliefs, recorded in our brains, are <u>like grooves on a record</u> that continually play a certain song. The lies that we believe and the patterns we live out have compounded over many years, carve deep grooves into our psyche.

   Romans 7:24-25: "O wretched man that I am! <u>Who will deliver me from this body of death?</u> I thank God—through Jesus Christ our Lord."

4. These lies then become mindsets and strongholds that are exceedingly difficult <u>to penetrate</u> with the truth. True and lasting deliverance is hindered because of a faulty belief system. The stronger the belief the deeper will be the groove.

Slide 3:

REPROGRAMMING THE BRAIN

1. God has created us with a spirit that when empowered to take its rightful place of dominance over the soul, is able through the Holy Spirit to <u>override these old beliefs</u>.

THE BRIDE MAKES HERSELF READY

2. New thoughts and beliefs of God's truth and life can then be imprinted in our consciousness.

   1 Corinthians 2:11: "For who among men knows the thoughts of a man except the man's <u>spirit within him</u>? In the same way no one knows the thoughts of God except the Spirit of God."

3. In the process of deliverance, we must work with God to <u>reprogram the false information</u> and un-Godly beliefs our brain has accepted over the years.

4. When we choose to submit to God's process, we <u>hasten the day</u> of our deliverance from sinful tendencies created by the lies we have believed.

5. Lets us now look at some important steps in the process of cleansing our souls, reprogramming our brains, and <u>changing our lives</u>.

___
___
___

Slide 4:

PUT THE AXE TO THE ROOT OF SIN

1. In the process of reprogramming our minds in righteousness, God must put the axe to the root of sin. Our first steps are to <u>identify and diligently root out</u> the weeds of un-Godly beliefs in our minds.

   Isaiah 61:11 "For <u>as the soil makes the sprout come up and a garden causes seeds to grow,</u> so the Sovereign LORD will make righteousness and praise spring up before all nations."

2. However, the timing for pulling out the roots <u>belongs to God</u> as revealed in the parable of the wheat and tares, where God said let them grow together for a time.

3. In the process of putting the axe to the root of sin, the Lord provides a formula that guarantees success in our transformation. The formula is to recognize, repent, resist and refuse. This formula works when we allow the Lord much room to work in the garden of our hearts.

___
___
___

Slide 5:

REPROGRAMMING THE BRAIN – RECOGNIZE

1. The first is to recognize: It is important to be able to <u>recognize the sin</u> that so easily besets us—the areas of weakness that continue to trip us up daily and the lies that undergird and sustain the sin (Heb. 12:1).

   Psalm 19:12-14 "Who can understand his errors? <u>Cleanse me from secret faults</u>. Keep back your servant also from presumptuous sins; let them not have dominion over me. Then I shall be blameless, and I shall be innocent of great transgression. Let the words of my mouth and the meditation of my heart be acceptable in your sight, O Lord, my strength and my redeemer."

2. Recognizing our sin and the lies that we believe is the very <u>first step</u> in the process of deliverance and for that, we sometimes need the help of the Holy Spirit.

3. The ability to recognize comes through the humbling of oneself. Pride sees all the flaws in others but <u>rarely sees itself</u>! We can grow in humility to recognize the patterns of sinful ways in our lives and understand the things that trigger our sinful responses.

4. Recognizing is a giant first step without which there will never be change or growth in Christ-likeness.

Slide 6:

REPROGRAMMING THE BRAIN - REPENT

1. The second step is to repent:

   Acts 2:38 "Then Peter said to them, <u>"Repent, and let every one of you be baptized in the name of Jesus Christ for the remission of sins</u>; and you shall receive the gift of the Holy Spirit."

2. The word remission in Greek is *aphesis,* which also means: <u>*pardon, freedom, deliverance* and *forgiveness.*</u>

3. Without repentance, <u>there is no remission of sins</u>. Repentance is the only avenue of escape from the prison of iniquity and the only means to cleansing and deliverance.

THE BRIDE MAKES HERSELF READY

4. It is important to remember that repentance is not simply <u>saying sorry</u>; it is also not justifying our sin or shifting blame.

5. Repentance is deep Godly sorrow and a willingness to change direction and turn away from sin.

   Matthew 3:8 tells us to: "<u>Produce fruit in keeping with repentance.</u>"

6. If we attempt to whitewash our sin, the sin becomes <u>protected and concealed</u> and there can be no possibility of deliverance.

7. There can be a large build-up from years of un-repented sin causing the foundation of our lives to be easily <u>shaken and oppressed</u>.

Slide 7:

REPROGRAMMING THE BRAIN - REPENT

1. Sin needs to be faced squarely and called what it is. Repentance requires a <u>deliberate choice</u> to turn away from sin and return to a right standing before God.

   Matthew 23:27: "Woe to you, scribes and pharisees, hypocrites! For you are like whitewashed tombs which indeed <u>appear beautiful outwardly</u>, but inside are full of dead men's bones and all uncleanness."

2. As we choose to align ourselves to God's way, the Cross becomes a part of our nature and we learn to grow in love and forgiveness.

Slide 8:

REPROGRAMMING THE BRAIN - RESIST

1. The third step to freedom is to resist. As we allow God a place to expose sinful ways that are hindering the progress of our destiny, we must seek the Lord for His strength to resist the compulsion and urge to give in to these ways. The Bible tells us in James. 4:7:

"Submit yourselves, then, to God. <u>Resist the devil, and he will flee from you</u>. Come near to God and he will come near to you. Wash your hands, you sinners, and purify your hearts, you double-minded. Grieve, mourn and wail. change your laughter to mourning and your joy to gloom. Humble yourselves before the Lord, and he will lift you up."

2. It is very important and crucial to our success that we understand clearly that we cannot <u>resist in our own strength</u>, as the outcome will be failure.

3. The enemy is not afraid of us; <u>he is afraid of Christ in us</u> who is our hope of glory. Again, it takes humility to lean upon the Lord and look to Him for strength and wisdom in times of need.

4. As we practice looking to the Lord for the strength to resist, with time, it will become our <u>first instinct</u>. His life in us will begin to increase and we will grow in the stature of Christ; in the process, the enemy is displaced, and our sinful ways are left behind like an old skin that we have shed.

Slide 9:

REPROGRAMMING THE BRAIN - REFUSE

1. Lastly, we must refuse to turn back to the old ways:

    Isaiah 50:7 "For the Lord God will help me; therefore I will not be disgraced; <u>therefore I have set my face like a flint</u>, and I know that I will not be ashamed. He *is* near who justifies me; who will contend with me? Let us stand together. Who *is* my adversary? Let him come near me."

2. Jesus set His face like flint to pursue <u>His Father's will</u>. We must also set our face towards God's will and refuse the temptation to sin and go down old roads again.

3. When we choose to agree with a lie and harbor <u>un-Godly beliefs</u>, we agree with satan and align ourselves with the enemy. It is imperative to our deliverance that we refuse to give the enemy any place in our hearts and any rights in our lives, our families and our homes.

4. The Lord could have led Israel out of the wilderness anytime He chose to, but the wilderness journey was designed by Him to test the heart and reveal <u>the truth of its condition</u>.

5. The people of Israel were given the opportunity to choose to humble themselves, repent and change their ways. An entire generation chose not to do so and died without receiving their <u>promised inheritance.</u>

6. We should be careful lest, by not allowing the Lord to change our ways and transform our hearts to one in which He is comfortable to dwell and make His habitation, we lose the promises inherent in our salvation.

7. The true measure of our faith in the Lord is <u>revealed in the test;</u> however, God will always give us the opportunity to repent and increase our faith in Him.

8. As we are transformed in the image of Christ, we will have His strength to refuse the old paths, and His <u>faith to stand</u>.

_____
_____
_____

Slide 10:

PLANT AND REINFORCE SEEDS OF TRUTH

1. To maintain our freedom, we must <u>plant and reinforce</u> seeds of truth and practice living in them.

2. For real and lasting change to take hold, it must begin at a deeper level of the thought processes. God's truth planted on the rich soil of humility will take root when watered and reinforced daily with <u>thanksgiving and praise.</u>

   Psalm 144:7-10: "Reach down from heaven and rescue me; rescue me from deep waters, from the power of my enemies. Their mouths are full of lies...<u>I will sing a new song to you, O God</u>! I will sing your praises with a ten-stringed harp. For you grant victory to kings!" NLT

3. We must truly begin to *sing a new song,* one that convinces the brain of a <u>*change of heart*</u> that will carve out new paths of *truth*. God encourages us in many places in His word to sing a new song—the suggestion is a change of heart and mind.

_____
_____
_____

Slide 11:

PLANT AND REINFORCE SEEDS OF TRUTH

1. To reprogram the brain, and to begin to <u>live empowered lives</u>, the truths of the Word of God must become the foundation of the lyrics of the new song we sing daily. We must fill our lives with God's word by reading it, eating it and singing it.

2. Place it on our walls, meditate on it and <u>ponder it daily</u>. Singing the Word is quite powerful in making a lasting impression on the brain and carving out new grooves of truth based on the word of God.

    Philippians 4:8: "Finally, brethren, whatever things are true, whatever things are noble, whatever things are just, whatever things are pure, whatever things are lovely, whatever things are of good report, if there is any virtue and if there is anything praiseworthy—<u>meditate on these things.</u>"

3. The Word of God is life and truth! We must live and eat it daily in order to maintain a life of humility and strength in God. As we dwell on what is good, true, and righteous, it is important to begin to <u>speak, live, and act free</u>.

4. As we are obedient to persevere and to overcome the obstacles on our path through faith, the day of deliverance *will come*—the day when we cross over into the land of promise and the Lord invites us to enter and <u>take possession</u>.

_____

Slide 12:

SING A NEW SONG

1. Our desired deliverance is united to the Lord as to where the Spirit of the Lord is, there is liberty and freedom! <u>God sings over us</u>, and He admonishes us to sing our praises to Him.

    Zephaniah 3:14 "Sing, Daughter of Zion; shout, O Israel! Be glad and rejoice with all your heart, O Daughter of Jerusalem!"

2. According to the Word, God inhabits our praises; praise has the power to change our mood and our beliefs <u>and makes a strong impression on the brain</u>—so, sing *a new song unto the Lord* (Zeph. 3:17, Ps. 22:3 2 Cor. 3:17). If you don't have a song just make one up based on truth!

3. See Appendix II for the Prayers of cleansing from Jezebel, Leviathan, Occult practices, and others. As you pray invite the Holy Spirit to lead you into healing, deliverance, and freedom. If you are doing the online course from our website, just click on the PDF icon to download the prayers.

_____

_____

_____

APPENDIX

CLEANSING PRAYERS

Prayer for Generational Curses:

Most Holy Father, I stand before You today in humility, I come by the way of the Blood of Your Son to seek your mercy. I ask Your forgiveness for myself and my forefathers, for our sin and rebellion to Your ways. We have not wholeheartedly obeyed Your commands and Your precepts and Word. We have trampled on the Holy Spirit's heart time and time again. Lord, I don't deserve Your mercy, but You are Good and Your mercy endures forever. Lord, I ask Your forgiveness and choose today to turn away from all sin.

I now renounce *and break agreement with all generational sin and traits; my sin/s of _____ in the generational line of my ancestors and now make a deliberate choice to turn away from sin walk in Your Ways. I place the Blood of Jesus between myself and my ancestors and close the door to the past and all generational iniquity.*

Cleanse me *Lord by Your great power, and in Your mercy break the power of iniquity that runs through the generations of my family. I choose to enter fully into my place in Jesus and receive fully the benefits of His Bloodline that washes, cleanses and delivers. Place the precious Blood of Your Son who died for my sins, on all the gates of my life. Seal my spirit with the Blood and be the Wall of fire that forever guards and preserves my life for Your Glory.*

I declare that *You alone are the Lord of my life, You are the Rock on which I make my stand, You alone will I serve all the days of my life with your strength and faith rising up in me daily. May my life be a praise to Your name and shine for the glory of Your Son that He may receive all the honor, praise and Glory due His great name. I love You Lord, Have Your Way.*

Prayer for Occult Curses:

Heavenly Father, I come before Your Throne of mercy today to ask your forgiveness for all the times in my life or my ancestor's lives when we have come into agreement with the kingdom of darkness and given worship to Satan directly or indirectly through practices that are an abomination to You.

Lord I ask forgiveness for myself and my ancestors and repent for allowing my mind and my soul to be defiled by the practices of _____

I Renounce *all the works of darkness and break agreement with all demons of the occult. In the Name of Jesus, the name above all names, I loose myself from the power of the enemy's hold on* *my soul and bind my life to the very Life of Jesus. I break the power of any generational curse that I have come under, through the power of the Blood of Jesus.*

Cleanse me *O Lord from all defilement and stench of the enemy. I acknowledge that You alone are God, that Jesus was triumphant and victorious over all the powers of the enemy at the Cross. I take my position in Jesus as a child of the living God and ask that You apply the precious Blood of Jesus to all my sin and wash me and make me clean in Your sight.*

I Declare *that Jesus is the King over all demonic kings and the Lord of lords that every evil king that has had influence in my life and a hold on my soul must loose it now in Jesus name; I declare that every curse is now broken by Jesus' awesome power.*

Prayer for Freemasonry:

Most Holy God, Great Judge of the Universe, I come before Your throne of mercy today to make my appeal. Lord, I ask forgiveness for myself and my ancestors for disobeying your word not to make vows. Forgive us for binding ourselves in a covenant of agreement with the powers of darkness by our word and by our actions through rituals that have ensnared our family in all generations, and made us captive to the Masonic Lodge, any secret society or fraternity and through any blood covenant.

I ask forgiveness for all un-Godly communication and dishonoring of Your Great Name and Your Word. I ask forgiveness for all declarations of worship to Baal, Ashtoreth, Allah or any other God or idol through oaths and vows I have taken or anyone in my family line.

According to Colossians 2:13-15, I now renounce and break agreement with all vows and oaths taken by myself or my ancestors; I renounce and break agreement with all idols, gods and goddesses, the power of all rituals, symbols and regalia in every degree, all Master Masons and pontiffs, false light, false unity and false sons of light, the false king of heaven, false father and son. I renounce and break agreement with all secret handshakes and secret words of every degree up to and including the 33rd and any presently unknown. I break agreement with astrology and the Zodiac, all animal behavior, all lies and deception not aligned to the Word of God, perverted sexual sin and all violence against the human body through all generations back to Adam.

Lord, break the curse of fatherlessness, isolation, sickness and disease on every part of my body including the mind. Lord, break the curse of demonic vision and deceptive revelation. Lord cleanse my mind and body from every trace of demonic defilement, wash me in the Blood of Jesus and make me completely clean and whole again.

Lord, I break every soul tie with every charismatic leader of the Masons and break every soul tie with the Masonic Lodge and all defiled land that Lodges occupy. I charge every demon with Fraud for attempting to collect on a debt already paid by Jesus and send you to Jesus now to receive what is your due.

Lord, I declare that there is only one God, the Lord God Almighty, who is merciful and faithful and causes us to inherit the generational blessings of godly parents to a thousand generations. Dear Lord, today I receive the blessing of being Your child, and the generational blessings from godly forefathers to a thousand generations, and I bless Your Holy Name!

Prayer for Cultic Religions:

Heavenly Father, most Holy God of Israel, I stand before your Throne of Mercy today as a sinner saved by your Grace and great Love. With Jesus as my advocate and defender, who pleads my case and lives to intercede for me, I make my petition today. I plead guilty for having bound myself in a covenant of agreement with the demonic king of the religion of_____. I humble myself before You Father and ask forgiveness for dishonoring the Gift of your Son's life given for me. Forgive me for rebelliously choosing to align myself with the lies and deceit of the powers of darkness and for having sinned against you.

Today I choose to renounce *all lies and ungodly beliefs of the religion of_____. I now break every tie with all spirits related to this religion. I plead the blood of Jesus over my soul, my mind, my heart and my spirit, and with Your authority and in your name Lord Jesus I command all demons of this religion and their practices to leave me now and go to You to be dealt with.*

Lord, I ask that in your supernatural power as my creator and the one who fashions me for your Glory, that you would cleanse all of me, to the deepest recesses of my soul and my thinking from every trace of defilement from this or any cultic religion I or my ancestors have been a part of. I desire to be wholeheartedly yours, that all of me would belong to you.

Thank you for your merciful goodness to me; keep me hidden in your pavilion and your embrace as you have promised in Your Word. I commit myself to you today to do your will and to embrace my life as a child of God and serve the only wise King—Jesus Christ. Amen.

Prayer for Jezebel & Leviathan:

Heavenly Father, please forgive me for allowing myself to be used by the spirits of Jezebel and Leviathan through words or actions, to bring harm in any way to the leadership You have placed me under, my church family, my immediate family and my friends. Forgive me for grieving Your heart and the Holy Spirit. In your great enduring mercy please deliver me now from the oppression and influence of these spirits.

Today I choose to renounce *and break agreement with Jezebel and Leviathan and turn away from the darkness to walk in the Light of the holiness of Jesus Christ. Lord, with Your authority and in Your power, I command Leviathan and Jezebel and every demon in their association, that thought they had found a home in my soul and my heart, to leave now and go to You Lord to be dealt with. Lord Jesus set me free to live and move and have my being only within Your life.*

Cleanse me *of all defilement from these spirits and remove the roots that have found a place in the land of my soul through my sin or that of my ancestors. Remove the image of Satan from me in Leviathan and Jezebel and conform me to the image of Your Son Jesus. Lord, apply the Blood of Jesus to my sin and to the gates of my soul that gave these spirits entrance and seal them forever in Your determination and will. I break the power of these spirits over my life now by Your Great Name, Your Blood and Your Power!*

Today I declare *Your Lordship and complete sovereignty over my life and my soul. I bring all my being under Your rule and reign O Precious King. Lord, in Your Holy Name, I now call my entire being, body, soul and spirit, into wholeness and complete health, and into the abundant Life that is mine in Christ Jesus.*

Other Courses from Headstone Academy:

FOR THE CAUSE OF ZION

The Law Will Go Out from Zion - The Word of The Lord from Jerusalem

Possessing an understanding that Israel is the central factor in the unfolding of God's end-time plan will become crucial for all the saints, especially pastors and leaders, working and partnering with God to enforce and complete His purposes. A deficiency in this understanding will become a handicap in the ability to process the movements of God. A proper understanding of this issue provides access to the keys to apprehend the fullness of His leading and direction, and the facility to be aligned with His plans in this hour in relation to our nation. Understanding of God's sovereign plan through Israel is vital to spiritual health and safety, for ourselves individually, and for the nations of the world.

There are many mysteries spoken of in the Bible that awaited God's opportune moment in history for its revelation. Paul speaks in Roman 11:25 about a mystery kept hidden—the partial hardening of Israel's heart until the set time of completion of God's work in the Gentiles. Revelations 10:7 shows that in God's divine timing the mysteries of God will be finished. In the twenty-first century, as antisemitism is on the rise around the world, including in the church, it seems that the truth of God's sovereign and eternal selection of Israel as the chosen place of His throne remains veiled to many.

CALL FOR THE WOMEN

Released in An Appointed Time for Maximum Impact

The vast number of women now being called forth and released into ministry and leadership roles within the Church and in the world, can be taken as a very powerful sign of the lateness of the hour in which we live, as women have been created to play a significant part in the work to prepare the way for the Lord's Coming.

We are the Headstone or Capstone generation, which means it is the time of summing things up in Christ in fullness and maturity in preparation for His Coming. Jesus will be coming in accelerated waves of His Presence before He returns. To whatever measure of His coming this generation is called to—and whether it is twenty or one hundred years till he returns, we must fully utilize the time with wisdom. God is now calling women to come forth "for such a time as this!"

Women are being called to the battle, whether to travail in the closet, on the front lines of the battle or in leadership roles in the House of God. It is vital that women are fully secured and grounded in their identity in Christ, as daughters of God. This Course unpacks revelation important to the release of women for their role in God's Kingdom Campaign for world Dominion.

Visit our store to purchase PDF Teacher's Manuals AR PURCHASE ON Amazon.com:

store.headstoneministries.com

Made in the USA
Monee, IL
29 September 2021